The Screening

The Screening

Mosadi Brown

Faith With Works Publishing
2014

First Printing: 2014

ISBN 978-0-9939024-0-6

Faith With Works Publishing
304-3 St Stevens Ct
Toronto, ON, M9A 3A9

Email: bmosadi@hotmail.com

Contents

Acknowledgements

I would like to thank my spirit guides and teachers, for the many experiences that inspired me to write this book. The content has also been inspired by the enlightenment garnered through applying the tools provided through Ronna Herman's book series – namely The Golden Promise and Scripting Your Destiny without whose help this book would never have been completed.

The jacket cover art has been provided courtesy of crystal angels: http://www.crystalangels.org.uk/

Chapter 1: Reflection

She reaches for and is amongst the stars. She had not yet incarnated onto the earth plane for another sojourn and was contemplating the value of her next lifetime. Sitting with her soul family she had reflected on the limitations and opportunities of the most significant experiences she had in previous incarnations. She pondered the pros and cons of all of her experiences and sat in wonderment and full of hope. She dwelled in her personal pyramid of light with her soul family in meditation of her thoughts and feelings. Recognizing that all of her thoughts and feelings both positive and negative were necessary for her highest outcome in the spiral of ascension. She quietly sat down in one of the crystal quartz chairs and allowed the twelve brilliant rays of the Creator to infuse her, balancing and harmonizing her energetic field in preparation for watching her previous experiences on a screen mounted in front of her and on the wall of the pyramid. The crystal quartz that protrudes from the capstone of the pyramid releases a stream of golden white light that shines down like a lightning bolt that pierces through the top of her light body charging her with the creative Source energy and filling her with love and positivity.

One of her guides says, "You have just been uplifted to a high vibration through the infusion of love/light energy. Reflecting on your prior life experiences what thoughts and feelings are impressed upon your mind?"

She responds, "I have not felt connected to Spirit and forgot to get quiet and to go inward for a source of security, love, worthiness, and validation. This led to much pain and suffering as I often felt a lack of vitality as well as feelings of unworthiness and being unloved."

Her guide asks, "Do you see how these feelings directed your choices and actions in your prior life experiences?"

"Yes," she answered. "I would try to please people through engaging in behaviours that I thought people wanted or trying to mold myself much like a chameleon to situations as a way to manipulate and control the outcome. Sometimes this would work and I would get the validation I needed to feel satisfied. More often the feeling of satisfaction would be temporary or I would not be able to control the outcome in a way that suits my desires and needs. This would lead to much disappointment, anger, and resentment. When I tired of behaving in such a calculating manner, I would become standoffish or distant, not let people in, and isolate; or, I would aggressively defend myself after thoughts and feelings built up enough and would project this outwardly and based on the belief that I do not measure up to other people's standards of me."

"Are there other areas of pain and discomfort that you can identify from your prior life experiences and at this stage in your spiritual awakening?" asked another angelic guide.

"Yes, I experience fear of showing vulnerability."

"Do you think this stems from false pride?"

"Absolutely! I often use illness to mask fear of showing vulnerability, for it is an excuse that has worked well in establishing and maintaining a safe distance from others. When others cannot get close they cannot hurt me."

Another guide responds, "Ah, so another example of how fear-based emotions and thoughts drive your actions on the earth plane. Are there any other sources of pain that you can identify?"

"Yes, I have feelings of unworthiness."

"Can you expand on that?"

"I feel unworthy of happiness, fulfillment, and freedom. When I experience rejection, disagreement, and discord in some way this confirms my negative self-image."

"How do these feelings control you through your choices and behaviours?"

"I avoid situations such as group gatherings and social events because I feel unworthy of establishing healthy and harmonious relationships with others. This also relates to feelings of unworthiness with respect to creating happiness, joy, and fulfillment in my relations with others. These feelings produce limitations in my ability to connect with others in an authentic and satisfying way. My actions follow suit to this because I either cancel opportunities to attend social or group gatherings; using illness is a part of this since it means that I do not have to participate."

"How do you respond when there is disagreement and discord with others when you do participate in group gatherings?"

"I judge or criticize others either inwardly or outwardly which creates even more of a distance between myself and others. Judging and criticizing is also a way that I mitigate the pain that stems from fear of being proven unworthy through other people's responses since I do not have to acknowledge their input which I take as the belief that they are overpowering me in some way. This also brings about a feeling of helplessness that is often unbearable."

"You describe experiencing a sense of inadequacy in your affairs, correct?"

"Yes. Also, fear from prior disappointments and hurt. This has blocked me from realizing my potential because my choices and behaviours are often driven by unhealthy and crippling thoughts and feelings."

Following this honest and poignant discussion about prior life experiences they all sit in contemplation, pondering what has just been communicated and reflected upon. As they lovingly sit together in silence, one of her angelic guides states, "You will be incarnating back into the third dimensional reality on the earth plane. Keeping in mind your description and the nature of earth school that humans are functioning mostly from instinct and a semi-aware state. You describe this in the beliefs you have acquired in your many years of experience. This includes feelings of being unloved, unworthy, a sense of helplessness, and many fear-based thoughts and emotions. These thoughts and feelings have driven your reaction to events through your actions such as anger, resentment, judgment and criticizing others as well as yourself, and standoffish tendencies."

Her second angelic guide intervenes and states, "The calculating behaviour or need to take on the role of a chameleon to please others drives a flow of events where you drift and coast based on events that are placed in your path. Through molding yourself to what you think others standards of you are, and therefore what you should be, you lose a sense of self, for as you say, you take on the role of a chameleon in your attempt at pleasing others to satisfy some inner desire or need you possess. This leads to a reactive approach to earthly life since you choose to accept what is thrown in your direction rather than selecting what you want. It has been easier for you to self-sacrifice, as you relinquish what makes you happy and instead focus on other people's desires and needs. Because you have become accustomed to living this way, you are pushed and pulled along the path of least resistance, which ironically contributes greatly to your pain and suffering."

Her third angelic guide observes, "When you are able to successfully get what you want from other people or other people are behaving in a way that you desire, this leads to temporary satisfaction. I say temporary because nothing on the earth plane is static. The physical realm is always changing, it is never the same. An obvious example is your physical vessel through aging. Your bodily functions slow down, and your outer appearance changes as you grow older in earthly time. This is an example of limitation in physical form since you exist within the limits of your physical vessel. This does not mean that you are limited internally; you only become limited internally when you identify what is happening externally and equate that with the standards you believe yourself to be internally.

This brings me to how you have viewed yourself in previous lifetimes. When you successfully manipulate the outcome from a place of trying to please others, you equate that with being happy within self. When the opposite happens and others are not responding in a way that you desire or need, you see yourself as a victim for you place your happiness and fulfillment in life in other people's hands. That is - you monitor how you are doing on the earth plane from sources outside of yourself."

One of her spiritual guides says, "Following what was just stated, you have experienced a lot of disappointment in a variety of forms. When there is a chance for happiness and fulfillment, fear takes over and you take on feelings of guilt. Therefore fear and guilt have driven your actions, and therefore your life experiences. As a result of fear and guilt you become preoccupied by shortcomings and a sense of failure. This draws the spirit of limitation to you as the universe will rearrange itself to fit your picture of reality. Following this is apprehensiveness about the future as you propel yourself within a sphere of consciousness imbued by fear and guilt that prevents you from moving along your life path in the way that you are meant to and that is your divine birthright."

Her other spiritual guide adds, "You possess all of the talents, virtues, and abilities to create a life of joy, peace, abundance, and love. This is your Divine Birthright. When you incarnate, you are veiled from the skills, talents, and abilities as you work to remember them through applying the tools you possess from within. When you begin to apply these tools, you start remembering who you are and then your life expands into freedom and grace. God does not punish, only presents us with the opportunity to wake up to who we are. This is why you descend into the denseness of physical reality, for these experiences are placed in your path for your highest growth. Then you transcend into a world of limitless potential where anything is possible. You can see clearly from your prior life experiences that you have just forgotten."

She responds, "Indeed."

One of the great Archangels comes into the pyramid of light now at the request of all gathered and through his sword of Divine Will, he re-qualifies and harmonizes any negative impacted energy that dwells within the pyramid.

He then asks, "Are you now ready for the screening? That is to view your prior life experiences to see the details of how your thoughts, feelings, and emotions created your reality so that you can see more clearly how these manifested in your circumstances with people, places, and things?"

"Yes, let us watch now."

"In this past incarnation you are known as Michelle, an older sister to Jennifer who lived in a two parent home. You married a man named Arthur and were a friend to a neighbor named Lucy. Through this viewing you will see that everyone has a part to play that provided an opportunity for your highest growth. All have been granted free will and therefore it is always your choice what you do with the lessons and opportunities that are presented to you. Remember that free will is a blessing from God. God does not punish; the limitations we experience come from within, thus we place limits on ourselves. It is always your choice as to whether or not you break the shackles of limitations and move into ease and grace."

"Okay, I understand."

One of her guides set the intention to begin the display of her prior life experiences on the screen and it began to display the audio and visual occurrences. Her soul family surrounded her with loving protection as she watched.

Chapter 2: The All Night Conversation

She was a loving older sister with whom her younger sister would come to for guidance and support. Her name was Michelle and her younger sister was named Jennifer. They would often stay up all night talking and contemplating the future direction of their lives. Jennifer was a school-girl who had a crush on a classmate and they recently began dating. She watched the screen with deep consideration becoming part of the visuals.

Jennifer expressed that although there was obvious mutual attraction she could not figure out why Christopher did not treat her like a lady. She would often say, "It does not seem to matter what I do, he does not seem to want to commit to me and he appears to have wandering eyes.

I have a hard time understanding his intentions because he communicates mixed messages. For example last week we went out for a nice long walk by the water and he had prepared this beautiful picnic lunch in the park. We decided to miss the rest of the day at school and sat in the park amongst the gardens laughing, talking honestly, and displaying our affections for each other. This week he is ignoring me and acting very aloof and distant.

He also seems to have an eye for Nancy who is supposed to be a good friend of mine. Despite this I feel like I cannot trust Nancy because she flirts with him – sometimes right in front of me. This has been going on for quite some time and it is a blatant disrespect. Christopher says that it is all in good fun and Nancy just brushes my concerns off stating that I am being insecure.

I do not know what to do sister. Can you help me?"

Michelle looked at her sister with empathy and yet was not surprised.

Michelle is soon to be married and is in awe that her sister would allow others to treat her this way.

"Sister I do not understand why you tolerate this. If Christopher truly cares for you then he will focus on courting you only."

"I know, but I cannot resist the energy that I feel between us."

"How did you meet him?"

"Christopher was involved in my orientation when I first started attending Lakeshore High School. He was involved in providing information about the first year classes and also the extra-curricular activities that exist within the school. He was an inspiration to me from the beginning because he gets decent grades and is a wonderful athlete. He is the star of the basketball team and track team. He also is a peer prefect and tutor because he excels at relating well to his classmates, particularly as it relates to peer pressure and how to transition well into the high school environment."

"Christopher sounds like he has been a good mentor to you, so why not keep the relationship focused on school-related endeavours?" asks Michelle.

"Well he is very pleasing to the eye, and his charisma is attractive to me," replies Jennifer.

"He also sounds like quite the ladies' man," observes Michelle. "How come you have not mentioned him that much up until now?"

"Well, things appeared to be going really well between us. Until Nancy intervened. We would study together; he tutored me in math and I could feel the chemistry building between us."

"What do you mean by chemistry?"

"We started out focusing on course work only. Eventually we started to talk about our future and what we hope to accomplish after high school. I was not sure about what direction I wanted to go in. Christopher told me that the crux of success in adult life is surrendering my desires to a relationship and to the male figure in my life. He said that love drives all and with love in my life, the sky is the limit."

"What about your own goals after high school and what you would like to achieve independent of a relationship?" inquires Michelle.

Jennifer ponders this for a moment and then says, "Christopher is great about encouraging me to focus on my studies. He believes that after high school, a woman's role is to look after her man. For in this way the man is charmed into providing the woman with all that she needs."

8

"What is Christopher's opinion about what a woman needs?"

"Love, romance, a secure home. Christopher believes that a woman's success in high school predicts her ability to succeed well in domestic activities later in life. I guess that is why he inspires me so much in the arena of relationships. He is very charismatic and has many friends and admirers. Many people look up to him, and admire his talents. A lot of girls at school have a crush on him and are practically hanging off of his every word."

"How does this make you feel?"

"Envious because I only want Christopher for myself. I feel that the only way I can have him is to follow what he tells me about women and how they should conduct themselves."

"What about what you want, Jennifer?"

"Christopher has talked me out of pursuing my desire to be a lawyer. He says that this will take away from my focus of being a loving wife whose responsibility is fulfilling her man's needs and wishes."

"So you are willing to not pursue something you are passionate about because of what Christopher tells you? Don't you think this is a risk to jeopardizing your own life passions?"

"Not if I have Christopher. I take on his opinions as my own. If I have him then that is enough to satisfy me in my life and life endeavours."

"What about Nancy? It seems that he is not as loyal to you as you are to him."

"Christopher says that part of a man's role is to rejoice in the affections of a variety of women."

"Do you have any other admirers?"

"Yes, sister, there is another man named Joe who likes me."

"What is he like?"

"Joe is really nice, he has been a good friend to me, and I feel like I can talk to Joe about anything."

"How does Christopher feel about Joe?"

"Christopher feels that I am not being lady-like by being friendly with Joe and that I should keep my distance since a real lady only focuses on one man at a time."

"Don't you think that is hypocritical? Especially in light of his tendency as you describe of having wandering eyes?"

"Christopher does not have wandering eyes, Nancy is just being annoying."

"Yes, but you just said that Christopher admitted to being receptive to the affections of multiple women."

"Yes, because he is gorgeous! Who wouldn't want to be with him?"

"Aren't you worried about losing his interest if he philanders? I sense that there is a double standard here."

"Whatever. Christopher has convinced me to sacrifice my career goals, and I am willing to do this if I have him and only him."

"What about Nancy? Why are you still friends with someone who is pursuing your crush?"

"Nancy is very popular at school. Being friends with her means I get to stay in the in-crowd."

"This is more important to you than having a loyal friend who treats you with respect?"

"Well when I have Christopher for my own, I will know that I have won and that I am superior to her. She is only pursuing him because he likes me the most and she is jealous."

"What makes you so confident that Christopher will choose you over Nancy?"

Jennifer is quiet for a moment, remembering her earlier experiences with Christopher. She then replies, "Christopher and I study in the library a lot. In the beginning it was always just him and I." Jennifer fondly remembers.

"What was this experience like?" Michelle asks curiously.

"At first, we would focus solely on school work. He had lots of great tips and tricks for completing my school work successfully while maintaining an active social life. He would describe the strategies he adopted that worked well for him like summarizing and paraphrasing notes; seeing the broader concepts and filling in the details later; using practical examples as a way of retaining the information acquired in the classroom; and engaging in discussions with the teacher and others both in and outside of the classroom. These are all brilliant suggestions that have made my school-work more manageable.

When we would talk about practical application of course content, our conversations began to include personal experiences. Christopher would talk about how he engages others through his charismatic nature by taking an interest in others and what is important in their lives. He does not believe in writing people off at a whim even when people disappoint him. This is why he has so many friends.

I would talk about my desire to have lots of friends and to be in a relationship. I expressed the importance of having love in my life.

Christopher would go on to advise me that when I find love it is important to accept the man for who he is, and for his attributes and deficits. Accept the man no matter what for this is the only way that I will acquire and maintain true love in my life.

He would go on to advise me about being a lady and to him, this means loyalty and sacrifice. For when I find true love I should put my own ambitions aside to satisfy the man's needs and wishes. This way I will win his heart and will be by his side free of distractions. He voiced that men are not meant to be monogamous and this is why he has so many admirers and it is acceptable for him to pursue them as he wishes. He said that when a man comes back to the same woman despite his other dalliances that this is a sure sign that she is his one and only.

As I took in and absorbed all he said and adopted his beliefs as my own, an attraction began to flourish. We started to meet daily and he would take me to the local sweet shop; therefore our interactions extended outside of the school environment.

He would hold my hand and caress my face, looking at me affectionately. One day in the sweet shop Christopher vocalized his feelings for me," Jennifer explained. Jennifer began to visualize and describe a fond memory of her and Christopher at the library.

"Jennifer, you are beautiful, smart, and I love studying with you," said Christopher.

"I feel about you in a similar way," replied Jennifer.

"You validate that it is okay to be me, and I must admit this is something I do not receive at home from my own family. You motivate me to come to school everyday and to be the best I can be. You listen to me and take my advice."

"It is because what you have to say is valuable and I am in awe of your strength, charm, and wit," said Jennifer fondly.

"Can I take you out more often? Maybe to a movie, or we can continue to come here?"

"Sure, I would love to spend more time with you outside of the library," Jennifer agreed.

"What will your parents think? They are probably protective given that you are still in high school especially about keeping male company outside of school," stated Christopher.

"I just won't tell them. My sister and I talk but I know she can keep a secret."

"It doesn't matter to you what they think?"

"No, as long as I have you, I don't care what they think. You are the one that said love is worth sacrificing everything for."

"You got it," Christopher responded with a wink.

"The only thing is that you will not be able to call my house as my parents do not like men calling without meeting them in person."

"What if I want to talk to you outside of school?"

"I don't know, maybe I can ask Nancy if you can call her and relay your messages to me. In this way we can connect outside of school without you having to call my house directly."

"Okay, I do like that Nancy is free to receive calls from whomever she chooses; too bad your parents aren't as open."

"Yes, well that is just the way it is in my house."

Jennifer snapped out of this memory in response to Michelle's voice bringing her back to her present location in her and her sister's bedroom.

Michelle looks at Jennifer and then asks, "Was this around time that you started seeing him during school nights?"

"Yes," Jennifer replied. "I appreciate you covering for me when I told mom and dad that I was going over to Nancy's to study," Jennifer continues.

"He would take me out with his friends, and they would egg me on about losing my virginity, as would Christopher."

"How did you respond to that?" asks Michelle.

"At first, it was all in good fun but then I started to feel pressured because Christopher was paying more attention to Nancy. When I would go over to Nancy's house, Christopher would stop by. There was one time when we had finished eating and Nancy went to do the washing up. Christopher offered to help her and I remained in the den reading over an assignment for the next day. I heard a lot of laughter coming from upstairs so I went to see what all the merriment was about. Christopher was standing beside Nancy drying the dishes as Nancy was washing them. Jennifer had again slipped into a visualization as she described the occurrence to Michelle:

Christopher said, "Nancy, you are so funny and entertaining. I admire that about you."

Nancy replied, "I know, it is one of my attributes. I can always make people laugh."

"Confident too, I find that very attractive."

Christopher reached to take one of the dishes that Nancy had just finished washing, caressed her hand and stared at her for a moment.

"I would love to be exposed to that more often."
I proceeded to clear my voice and walked into the kitchen.

"Christopher, I think it is time for you and I to leave. It is getting late."

"Of course," Christopher replied. "Let me just get my things from the den."

I waited by the door for Christopher to gather his things. Nancy followed him downstairs and I could her them chatting and laughing.

"Christopher!" I shouted.

"Be right there," he shouted back.
He emerged from the den and Nancy followed him.

"We'll see you tomorrow Nancy."

"Yes, you will," she replied smugly.
Jennifer snapped out of the visualization and re-focused her attention on Michelle's question:

Michelle stared at her sister and then asked, "Didn't you see this as a red flag that he may not be the man for you, since this is an example of him treating you poorly?"

"I didn't see it that way. I only saw Nancy as a threat and it became a source of competition for me to win him over any way that I could."

"And then what happened?" asked Michelle.

"Well then we would continue to study in the library, only Christopher began to talk about Nancy more often. When she would walk by with our group of friends, he invited Nancy to join us, instead of just greeting her as she passed by.

For awhile, the three of us would study and Nancy would often joke and make comments that Christopher would find amusing. He began to pay less attention to me and I began to feel left out. I resented this deeply.

I wanted to stay within our circle of friends so I went along with Christopher and Nancy flirting with each other while I stood by in silent fuming. I would continue on denying what was happening because I did not want to be ostracized from the group even though I viewed Nancy as a threat. "

"How could you endure this intolerable behaviour?" asks Michelle.

"Well despite my perceived threat, having Nancy as a friend remains important to me because of all the fun associated with it. I get to go to social gatherings, there is a lot of attention paid to us, and I don't think that I could be happy without having our circle of friends, and all of the really cute male admirers. I always feel in the loop, plus Nancy has great fashion sense and gives great fashion advice."

"Oh, I see. So what happens next?" Michelle asks in anticipation.

"One night we all decided to hang out and go to a movie. We went out for pizza afterwards. Nancy and Christopher kept exchanging witty comments, and I could feel the attraction between them. Everyone was drinking beer except me because it was a school night. Christopher kept telling me that I was being boring because I wasn't drinking beer with them. I felt really alienated because everyone was connecting with each other except me. Christopher was also paying more attention to Nancy than me."

The boys started talking about amorous encounters with their girlfriends and Christopher said, "Well lucky for you boys," he glanced over at me nonchalantly.

Nancy countered with, "I am no stranger to amorous activities."

This generated much attention from everyone at the table. I replied, "Yeah right Nancy, you are just as much of a virgin as I am."

"Don't be so sure about that," sneered Nancy. "I can hold my own when giving men what they desire. That is more than I can say for you."

"I pulled back, afraid of confrontation as the boys gaped at her. We stayed at the pizzeria for awhile longer while I sat in envy of Nancy's ability to captivate the boys, and particularly Christopher with whom she was flirting with all night. Actually she was flirting with all of the boys and this seemed to really turn Christopher on."

"This really seems to be getting worse and worse," Michelle interceded as she listened to Jennifer's description of the occurrences at the pizza parlour.

"Well after we left the pizzeria I asked Christopher what I could do to keep his attention," Jennifer continued.

"Let me drive us to the lake, and you can show me." Christopher said.

"What do you mean?" responded Jennifer.

"You'll see," responded Christopher.

We drove to the lake, and Christopher pulled out a case of beer that he had stored in the trunk of his car.

"Common Jennifer, don't be a party pooper."

"But we have school tomorrow."

"So what? You have me to rely on to provide you with guidance and direction to succeed in your studies. Have I not always come through for you in the past?"

"Yes, you have," Jennifer agreed.

"Well then, what do you have to worry about? Remember what I told you. You must be willing to do what it takes to keep your man's attention."

"Okay."

Back in the sister's bedroom, Michelle asks:

"So you drank beer that night? Jennifer I must say that I am disappointed in you. How could you surrender to peer pressure like that?"

"I will do anything for Christopher. Including satisfying his amorous needs. It was that night that I lost my virginity, desperate to keep him away from Nancy. I also admire Nancy's confidence in captivating the boys and wanted to emulate what she does, especially given what she had said that night about her own sexual pursuits which I was not previously aware of."

"Don't you think that she was trying to manipulate you?"

"Maybe so, but I was consumed by the events of that night, and did not want Nancy to hook her claws into my boyfriend. After all we share many admirers and she has plenty of boys to choose from," Jennifer replied and resumed her flashback and description:

"After a few beers, Christopher reached over and kissed me. He lifted my blouse over my head and slipped his hand under my bra. I felt a jolt of energy go through me like a wave of electricity."

"I want you so much Jennifer. Don't be afraid, just let go."

"And so you went along with his agenda?" Michelle asked.

"Yes, and mine," countered Jennifer. We kissed passionately and he guided my hand toward the fly of his pants. I felt his prick and he pushed the seats back. He gathered all of his weight on top of me and I felt a sharp pain as it went in."

"Ouch, that hurts," I yelped.

"Just relax," Christopher said. "You feel so good."

"He penetrated back and forth inside of me, covering my mouth with his hands. After a few minutes it was over."

"A few minutes?" stated Michelle in disgust. "That does not sound like an ideal first time to me, and in his car to boot. What happened with Nancy after this occurred?"

"Well Christopher drove me home and told me how proud of me he was, and how brave he thinks I am. He said that I had won his affections forever.

Christopher continued calling Nancy for the purpose of relaying messages to me. Christopher and I continued to have intimate relations. Early on and right after I had lost my virginity to Christopher, he was back to giving me his undivided attention. Gradually things began to change as I would see him talking to other girls after school. He would tell me that these were just innocent interactions with girls who were looking for a study partner or were interested in his sporting activities. I felt very possessive and like I always had to fend them off. One day one of the girls from the debating club approached me and said, "You know, Christopher is super smart. We had a wonderful chat last night at Nancy's party."

"Wait a minute, Nancy had a party?"

"Yes, I thought you knew. Funnily enough, Nancy did not seem to mind that Christopher wanted to drive me home."

"He drove you home?"

"Yes, he has driven a few of us home on more than one

occasion. But don't worry, I know he is your guy. I just like to have fun."

"What is that supposed to mean?" Jennifer asked angrily.

"Nothing, I just thought I would let you know how lucky you are. Enjoy it while it lasts."

"It sounds like he was really making the rounds with the ladies. How did you respond?" Michelle asked.

"I sat back passively for a few months as Christopher and Nancy would gradually return to flirting with each other more and more. I internally started to build up hatred toward Nancy."

"Yet, you still stay friends with her," replied Michelle.

"Yes, oddly enough the more she betrayed me as a friend, the more I wanted to stay friends with her. Part of me wanted to defeat her and triumph over their undeniable attraction for each other.

One day, I went over to Nancy's house as she had left one of her books in the library. I had some time so I walked over there after school. Earlier that day, I was looking for Christopher and couldn't find him anywhere. Nobody knew where he was. Nancy was not around either and I had an uneasy feeling.

When I arrived at Nancy's house, her parents were still at work. Usually the door is locked; this time the door was open. I had called out Nancy's name a couple of times and there was no response.

I heard muted voices and moved toward the noise which was coming from upstairs. When I arrived at the top of the stair case, I could hear moaning and tip toed across the hall to see what was happening.

Nancy's bedroom door was propped open slightly, and I could see her and Christopher on Nancy's bed stark naked and humping like rabbits. Needless to say I was devastated, but knew this was coming eventually.

I left without letting either one of them know what I had saw and brought Nancy's book home with me."

"That would explain the night you were in tears and stayed home from school the next day sick," said Michelle.

"Yes, I could not bring myself to let anyone know. I just laid in my bed in misery. Nancy had called that night."

"Yes, I remember taking the call and passing the phone on to you. I could feel the awkwardness."

"You're not kidding. Nancy could sense it too and asked what was wrong. I had replied that nothing was wrong and that I was just not feeling well. I told her that I had her book that she left at the library."

Jennifer began to hear the conversation in her mind as she continued to describe it:

"Thanks," replied Nancy. "How is Christopher?" Nancy continued.

"Fine, things couldn't be better," Jennifer replied.

"I bet, he is certainly endowed with many talents," said Nancy.

"Yes, he is," replied Jennifer.

"We hung up the phone, and I cried and cried yet had in my mind that I was going to win both of their affections back no matter what it took."

"Wow, Jennifer. I am so sorry you have had to go through all of this," Michelle lamented.

Jennifer pondered this then replied, "Nancy always wants what I have."

"What do you have?" asked Michelle.

"A future with Christopher, and popularity at school."

"It sounds like it may be the opposite since she swapped your boyfriend and you said that you have chosen to stay friends with her because of her popularity."

"Yes, well it works both ways. As long as Christopher stays with me, I am sure he will tire of Nancy eventually. I just need to keep following his advice to stay loyal no matter what and to keep being a lady. When he sees how committed I am to him, he will run back into my arms. Especially given that Nancy has been clear about not being loyal. This way, he will direct his full attention back to me.

As for Nancy, by not writing her off, I still get to be with the in crowd at school in addition to all of the attention that goes along with it. Plus, I can still go to all the great parties."

"Do you want to know what I think after you have told me all of this?" asks Michelle.

"Of course," replies Jennifer.

"From what you have described, both Christopher and Nancy often cross the line because they can. I see that you enable them to do this out of some misguided sense of belonging, they see this, and therefore get away with their behaviour.

If you are truly okay with this series of events, then I do not think that you would take this much time to talk to me about it. It is no wonder then that you are in this current situation," states Michelle.

"So what are you saying?" asks Jennifer.

"Honestly?"

"Yes, honestly."

"If I were you I would speak with both of them and communicate clearly what it is that you want in addition to communicating what you will and will not tolerate. If they do not respect your wishes then I think it is best for you to eliminate them from your life and move forward. You deserve to be treated with the upmost respect and caring, and I think that you know this," advises Michelle.

"Well, like I said, I think I have my priorities straight. I just needed someone to hear me out since I have been internalizing everything," Jennifer says.

"Well I don't think it is all worth it if you are giving up your integrity and self-respect. Plus I have to keep covering for you when you stay out late."

"You still will cover for me, won't you sister? If you truly care for me and what is important to me."

"I suppose," sighs Michelle.

Michelle went silent feeling exhausted from this conversation. The truth is that Michelle could relate to Jennifer's descriptions more than she chose to vocalize. Michelle had her own set of insecurities pertaining to relationships in general. Unlike Jennifer, Michelle was more discrete about her insecurities because she was far more concerned with appearances, and being a role model amongst those with whom she interacts. It was important for her to display outwardly that she is the stability within the family, always there for those that need her. She thought about this obligatory pull that created much anxiety within her. For she desperately wanted to instill happiness in Jennifer and fix the situation that Jennifer had described. They both gradually fell asleep in the early morning hours; they had talked for most of the night.

Chapter 3: The Next Day

Both sisters woke up to find that both parents were not at home. Michelle had become accustomed to this over the years. They had been out at a party the night before leaving Michelle to look after all domestic activities, and to ensure that Jennifer is seen off to school.

Michelle often felt frustrated regarding her parent's irresponsible behavior. They always appeared to take advantage of Michelle's acts of kindness, and generosity. Michelle was very concerned most of the time and felt responsible for everyone in the home. She feels as if the roles have been reversed and that she is the parent taking care of her parents and younger sister. This has created a level of deep-seated resentment in Michelle for she feels that everybody else in the home gets to have fun and enjoy their lives at her expense.

Michelle is of the belief that it is not lady-like to speak up about her concerns and so often sits in silence with feelings of unhappiness and longing for things to be different.

Michelle proceeded to make Jennifer's lunch and helps her pack her school bag. Jennifer sighed in exasperation before leaving for the day.

"What is wrong?" asks Michelle.

Jennifer replies, "I have this assignment due by the end of this week for my English class and I have never acquired a knack for writing. Could you help me with my essay upon my return from school?"

Michelle hesitates as this is not the first time that Jennifer has procrastinated in her schoolwork, leaving assignments at the last minute and then expecting Michelle to pick up the pieces to help her out. Moreover, Michelle needs to visit her tailor to get her wedding dress fitted, work on wedding invitations, and she has not had much time to spend with her fiancée to discuss and continue to plan their wedding.

Michelle is also distraught because her parents have not supported her much in this endeavor. Michelle feels deeply disappointed as this is supposed to be one of the most special occasions in her life and her parents do not seem to care. Instead they go out on the town regularly and put their needs before hers. She feels saddened as she thinks about this.

Despite this Michelle musters up a smile and says, "Yes, I will help you with your assignment. Now go off to school and I will see you tonight."

Jennifer obeys as she hears a honk outside and begins to leave, "Oh there is Christopher!" Jennifer states, then goes on to say, "He is so sweet to give me a ride to school." It is as if their conversation the night before did not happen. Michelle smiles meekly and wishes her sister a good day at school.

Michelle begins to clean up the home awaiting her parent's return. As she is cleaning she reflects on the conversation with Jennifer the night before and tries to put things into perspective. Her sister longs to fit in and will do anything to gain approval from her peers. She is willing to go to any lengths to achieve this including shameful, guilt-ridden acts that compromises her self-respect. Nancy is someone she admires and looks up to because she is a part of the in crowd and goes after what she wants no matter how immoral. She appears to know what she wants and will manifest this through her thoughts and actions. This reflects in her popularity, and multiple suitors. She is an attention-grabber and succeeds in this through all of her assertions. Nancy's circle of friends succumb to her talent of manipulating others for her own personal gain. This misguided direction has lead her friends to blindly follow her words and beliefs regardless of whether or not they harm others. Jennifer is a part of this group and feels a need to follow blindly no matter what the consequences are because it provides her with a sense of identity and belonging.

Christopher is also someone Jennifer admires because of his charismatic nature. He too manipulates but in a different way. Through his looks, popularity, character, and convincing nature he manipulates Jennifer into thinking that he will provide her with all that she needs. Based on Jennifer's descriptions there is a need to feel loved, to get a sense of vitality, and to not feel lonely. Jennifer feels that she is loved by Christopher because of the attention that he provides. He provides this through physical means, convincing

Jennifer to lose her virginity as a way of seizing his love. Despite suggestions of the opposite through his wandering eyes, Jennifer believes that she seizes his love every time his attention turns back to her. When Christopher does not get what he wants, he turns his affections toward other women. She takes on his belief that it is because she is not interesting enough for him, and is willing to do whatever it takes to re-capture his attention through taking on what he believes to be interesting rather than standing in her own integrity. Jennifer's integrity has been compromised because she always said prior to meeting Christopher that she would hold out consummation until a man commits to her and only her and displays this through his actions. Christopher has demonstrated non-commitment through gaining affection from more than one woman because he likes the attention; this is not an act of love. Jennifer has inadvertently agreed to take on his belief system in order to fulfill his need for attention rather than focusing on what she values. This includes compromising her future endeavours to succeed independently because she has adopted Christopher's picture of reality that a woman's place is to stand by her man, no matter what, and regardless of the way the man treats her.

Jennifer feels alive when she is with Christopher and therefore places her ability to thrive in his hands. She also relies on Christopher for her own happiness, because she is convinced that when he is happy it is because she is being interesting and capturing his attention and also has this sense that she is no longer alone. He has convinced her of this. It is as if she needs Christopher to feel whole and complete, and feels alienated otherwise. When he threatens Jennifer with a break-up, she cannot stand the sense of abandonment, and will equate it with her own failure rather than seeing that she can do better by cutting her losses and moving on. She has been completely misguided. This saddens Michelle.

Michelle continues with the chores when she hears the door open and then slam shut. Her parents stumble in looking disheveled.

"Did you have a good time?" asks Michelle.

Michelle's mother – Gail – responds, 'Yes we did. Thank you for being a doll and looking after Jennifer last night."

Michelle's father looks at her sternly and asks if his boots and shoes have been polished for they still look soiled.

"I thought you were going to do this last night Michelle. I have an engagement today and you know how busy my schedule is."

Michelle looks at her father and responds, "I did polish them, but was rushed preparing dinner for Jennifer and trying to get her into bed at a decent hour."

Her father replies, "Well you have not done a good job. Do it again, and properly this time." He then proceeds to his office and shuts the door.

Michelle begins to re-polish her father's shoes looking anxiously at the clock as she needs to get to her tailor and finish cleaning the house.

Her mother is speaking despondently about a neighbor named Lucy who often gossips and is concerned about how she speaks ill of Jennifer in addition to the comments she makes about her and her husband. "I do not understand why Lucy is so adamant about being a busybody where Frank and I are concerned in addition to your sister," Gail states with annoyance. "Frank and I have an active social life, and your sister is impetuous. It is none of her business."

Michelle looks at her mother with a sympathetic expression. Her mother asks, "The next time she chatters on – could you have a word with her? I think you are the only one in this family who is capable of reasoning with her. You are after all the rock in this family and I do not have the energy nor the desire to engage in conversation with her."

"I'll try," responds Michelle. Michelle then asks, "Mother are you available to go with me to the tailor today? I am pondering the cut and fit of my wedding dress and am thinking of making subtle changes to the style."

Her mother responds, "Your father and I have another commitment to attend to Michelle. You know how busy we are. Why don't you ask your sister to go with you?"

"I'll ask her," says Michelle, feeling disappointed.

Frank emerges from his office smoking a pipe. He stands in the common room sighing in exasperation.

"Are you okay dad?"

"I just received an unpleasant call from a colleague."

"Is there anything I can do?" Michelle asks.

"I don't know, it seems like my colleagues only call when they want something. It doesn't seem to matter what I do, they are never satisfied, it would be nice if they appreciated me every once in awhile."

"I'm sorry dad, know that I appreciate you."

"Well, I would feel appreciated if you do as I say. Are you finished polishing my shoes?"

"Almost dad."

"Well, hurry up, I have much to attend to and I need those shoes polished now."

"Okay dad I am working on it." Michelle returns to the foyer to finish polishing her father's shoes.

Michelle gazes up at her parents. Her mom is sitting quietly staring off, and her dad sits down beside her mom, continuing to smoke from his pipe.

"I am going to the dress shop today dad, I was just telling mom that I will need help with the fitting and the design of the dress."

Her father looks over at her and does not appear to be interested.

"Fine." He responds. "While you are out could you pick up some tobacco for me?"

"Sure." Says Michelle.

"Common Gail, get your coat and purse, we are going out now."

"Another work engagement?" asks Gail. "I am excited to meet your new boss."

"Yeah, yeah, another asshole, another dollar. Just be the trophy wife you are and get your things will ya? You wouldn't have much of a life without these events I drag you to."

"I will Frank. Jennifer is going to help Michelle with her dress details."

"Well good, it means I don't have to worry about anything but putting food on this table. Someone has to pay for these bloody expenses."

"You provide for us well Frank," says Gail.

"I know, now hop to it, we have to go!"

"Okay, okay, calm down."

Gail goes upstairs to freshen up. Frank begins reading the paper while he is waiting.

Michelle ponders whether or not to tell her parents about Jennifer and the experiences she is having at school and with the people with whom she is involved with.

"Dad, can I talk to you for a moment?"

"What is it Michelle?" Frank looks over at her with an annoyed expression.

"I think that Jennifer may be in trouble at school."

"Why, are her grades failing?"

"No, it involves a boy, and also her group of friends."

"Well, it sounds like girl problems. You just continue to look after her, that is your responsibility as the older sister. I really don't have time to do deal with silly high school issues. Jennifer will be fine. It is as your mother said, Jennifer is impetuous. At least she has passion, something that I wish I saw more of in you."

Michelle looks at her dad feeling disappointed that he refuses to hear her out. "I...I.." stammers Michelle, starting to tell him about their conversation last night.

"Are you done up there yet?" Frank interrupts and shouts upstairs to Gail in impatience.

Gail comes downstairs in a hurry, "Sorry Frank, I am ready now."

"Good, finally. You both drive me nuts. Don't you see I am pressured here. I don't need to be encumbered by silly female issues."

"What are you talking about Frank?" asks Gail.

"Nothing, Michelle is just complaining about Jennifer."

"What's going on with Jennifer?" asks Gail.

Michelle has butterflies in her stomach, and decides to not say anything because she can feel the pressure of her father wanting to leave and wanting to get where he needs to go. Besides, her father often interrupts when Michelle tries to speak her mind.

They both hastily grab their coats, and her father snatches his shoes from Michelle's hands.

"Common, let's go," barks Frank. He continues, "Michelle, make sure that your sister doesn't chat too much with Lucy – that is if you both run into her at the dress shop. I don't need gossip spreading like wild fire in this neighbourhood."

"Of course, dad," quavers Michelle, fighting to hold tears back as her parents leave. "When will you be back?"

"Not sure, but we know you will manage things here just fine."

The door slammed behind her parents firmly and there was a haunting silence in the house. Michelle went over to the sofa and sat down in despondency. Thinking about her parents disregard for her needs and feelings was an ongoing burden she shouldered.

Michelle thought about the relationship that her parents had to each other and to her. She could see that her mother had a traditional view of family, living the need to be married, with children and to live within a home and a family. She lived by her parents assertion that a woman should be married by the age of twenty-one, and if she wasn't then she was a spinster. Within the marriage, it did not matter what the circumstances were, once married, it was frowned upon to leave, particularly when there are children involved. She had a need to hang in there no matter what and regardless of whether or not she was fulfilled in the relationship. Her mother was often very quiet and reserved, not really speaking what she was thinking or feeling, but rather just rolling with whatever came into her path. To avoid conflict she would often internalize much of what was going on and appeared to have this perpetual internal conflict. She needed to hang on to her immediate family as it fit her need for tradition and living the traditional way of life. Unfortunately for Michelle this lead to a conflict of interest because it also meant internalizing her thoughts and feelings when Michelle expressed a need to be listened to, considered, and heard. Michelle felt that her mother did not listen or pay attention when Michelle needed it, and instead, distracted herself with just about everything in her immediate surroundings in order to avoid being present with Michelle. It gave Michelle the impression that her mother was not interested in significant occurrences in her life. She instead focused on her own needs and a desire to fit the standards from the outside about what a family life should look like. She often used this self-image, which was largely dependent upon being married and having children as a crutch so that she did not have to face her internal conflict.

Then Michelle proceeded to think about her father. Her father was a very proud man. He was fixated on having things his way and would manipulate others as a means to achieve this. He was bright and has a very quick mind, yet often uses this as a way to control the outcomes of things. His sense of self-worth often came from successfully telling others what to do, and asserting his opinions both positive and negative. His resiliency and strength carried him through many situations and would use these attributes to persistently get his way.

Coming together, Michelle, can see how their attributes compliment each other, they fit each other's needs. Her the passive side of the coin, and him the aggressive side of the coin. They weren't all bad, yet they were so consumed with pride, and self-righteousness that they did not see how suffocating this could be for Michelle. In both cases, the relationship that Michelle had with her parents meant that all of her life she has been unable to flush out her own feelings about the events in her life. Michelle knew that this was not an option for her and that her role is to be the rock of the family. To be strong no matter what, and to ensure that everyone else's needs in the family were met. This would extend to her husband once they are married. Despite the despondency, Michelle felt comfortable in her role as 'the rock of the family' because it meant that she could focus her attention in the way that she always has, and therefore has become accustomed to. She could not imagine living her life in any other way. For then, what would she be responsible for? What would her role in life become? She shuddered at the thought.

Michelle sighed in exasperation as she thought about the dynamics in the home. She felt alone and abandoned. This saddened her deeply.

As Michelle was finishing up the cleaning the phone rang.

"Hello?"

"Hello beautiful, it's Arthur," he said cheerfully on the other end of the phone.

"Oh hello stranger, you have good timing," said Michelle excitedly.

"Why, what's up?" asked Arthur.

"Well, my parents just left the house, and I was just thinking that it is yet another pass through as they jaunt off to their next set of activities. It means that I have to continue to look after Jennifer, and tend to the house in their absence."

"Yes, but you are used to it now right?"

"I guess."

"You are a strong lady, I am sure it is no skin off of your nose."

"So when are you coming back from your business trip?"

"Very soon, that is why I am calling. I cannot wait to see you!"

"I cannot wait either Arthur. It is great news that you are coming back soon."

"How are the wedding plans coming along?"

"Good, I just wish that you could be here for more of it so that we can share the experience together."

"Yes, well you know that I am busy working to provide us with everything that we need. Your father would have a fit otherwise, and may not permit me to marry you."

"I know, but it can get lonely sometimes."

"Well, you are bright and resourceful, and everything will be great."

"I hope so."

"It will be. Listen, I have to go now but I will see you really soon okay?"

"Okay."

Michelle hung up and wished that she had mustered up the courage to talk to Arthur about the conversation that she had with Jennifer last night. For some reason, Michelle felt a certain degree of awkwardness talking to Arthur about Jennifer even though it felt good to express herself more openly about her family. It seemed to Michelle that Arthur was often comparing the two sisters; Michelle felt that Arthur loved her and would never do anything impertinent where Jennifer was concerned but it seemed that when they were all in the same room together, Arthur let loose more and seemed more light-hearted. Michelle envied Jennifer's ability to bring that out in people as it is an attribute that Michelle knows that she has deep down inside, and is murked by her need to fulfill her responsibilities.

Arthur has often said that Jennifer would be a fun choice because of her playful and spontaneous nature; however, his real need is for someone more stable, soulful, and level-headed. He appreciates the stability as opposed to the volatile nature of Jennifer's pursuits since he believes this will reflect in their future home together, and as the future mother of his children. Michelle smiled to herself thinking about her future prospects with her fiancée and is excited to finally have her own home and life apart from her immediate family. She felt that she had paid her dues and it was finally time for her to go out on her own with the man she loves. She fantasized about this prospect from stable daughter, to stable wife, knowing the one thing that she could expect is that her role would remain the same, albeit with someone who appreciates her virtues in a different way. The thought of her future lifted her up into the clouds and she was glad that she could create this pleasurable story in her mind to escape the issues that she is integral to in her current family situation.

The day wore on, and Michelle did not realize how quickly time was passing. Reality flooded back, and she decided not to wait for her sister's return from school. She decided that she would go to the dress shop on her own for she had the feeling that Jennifer would be detained with Christopher and was unsure when her sister would turn up. She got up from the sofa, bundled up, and packed her things in preparation for heading to the dress shop.

Chapter 4: The Dress Shop

As Michelle heads to the dress shop she sees a number of acquaintances who breeze by her. These are people she has known for awhile who are otherwise friendly and yet do not offer to give her a ride on this nippy day. She has yet to understand this, as she knows in her heart of hearts that she would not hesitate to give any one of them a ride plus she has always been friendly and supportive toward them. At least she is getting her exercise she thinks to herself and plods on.

As Michelle walks along she thinks about her immediate family and wishes that someone was joining her today. She often felt neglected by her family: her father she thought was a very self-centred man and was hardly there for Michelle when she needed him. Instead he would always place his needs and individual interests first. Her upcoming wedding is a life event after all and despite this he still manages to find excuses for leaving her feeling disheartened and disappointed. As for her mother she felt sorry for her as she felt that her mother's kindness was often taken advantage of. It would be great to have a mother – daughter occasion shopping together, having her there for Michelle's fitting and admiring and indulging in the purchase of excessories. She felt twinges of guilt and shame whenever she thought of her mother in a negative way because she knows that her mother means well; but is preoccupied with satisfying everyone's wishes and needs in the home. As for Jennifer, well, girls will be girls. She knows what it is like to have a first love and understands the appeal of the romance and drama surrounding her experiences with her social circle and with Christopher as taking precedence over just about everything. Hopefully with time her priorities will change. Michelle was so engrossed in her thoughts that she almost walked by the dress shop. She began to feel butterflies in her stomach as she walked in.

Michelle walked toward the merchant. She felt as if she had shackles around her ankles and that she was walking in quick sand. She really did not understand why she felt this way because this is supposed to be an exciting time for her. Despite all of her misgivings, Michelle loves Arthur and is in great anticipation of starting a family of her own. She finally arrived at the counter after what felt like eons of time.

"Can I help you?" asked the merchant.

"Yes, I am here to pick up my wedding dress and to have it fitted. Here is my ticket," Michelle replied.

The merchant walked to the back of the store and through a set of curtains. Michelle waited intently.

"Is everything okay back there?" Michelle asked after waiting several minutes.

"Yes, sorry for the wait," the merchant shouted back. "I am just reading a note from the tailor attached to the tag of your dress. She will be in soon so that you can also have your fitting today. I will bring the dress out momentarily."

"Sure," Michelle responded. She began to walk around the store looking at all of the pretty articles of clothing and accessories. She had not had time previously to walk around this shop and take a good look around. She was awestruck at the variety of fabrics and of all the pretty colours and patterns. She walked from rack to rack, taking her time pouring over each article of clothing and accessory. Now that she was out for awhile she was beginning to enjoy time away from the house and from all of her obligations.

As she continued to browse the tailor emerged from the back of the store.

"Michelle, darling, how are you?"

"Fine, Jane, how are you?"

"Oh, you know, busy as ever! It seems like everyone wants their fittings at once. When it rains, it pours."

"Ah, yes, I understand. Jane, I was wondering…" Michelle paused in hesitation and then continued, "I was looking around at your selection and cannot help but to wonder if maybe there could be some adjustments made to the fabric. I was a bit rushed when making my selections the first time around and did not fully appreciate all that you have to choose from here."

"What did you have in mind?"

"Well, initially I thought the winter white ball gown style was suitable to my taste. I also thought the lace to be becoming to my style, and its extension into the straps, and the matching veil. After looking around I think that I prefer the mermaid style, as I think it is more flattering to my figure. Plus it is a stunning cut in my opinion. I also like that the mermaid style dress is strapless because I am thinking that one of your necklaces, particularly with the princess-cut stones would be a beautiful addition that matches this dress style better. I am also thinking of removing the veil and replacing it with specs of dainty embellishments etched throughout my hair within an up-sweep style."

The merchant gazed at Michelle, then turned around and muttered something.

"What, sorry Jane I did not hear what you said just then."

"Well…I," Jane said hesitantly.

"What is it Jane?"

"With the amount of time we have, I don't think it will be possible for me to accommodate your requests."

"Really? This would mean a lot."

"How would Arthur feel about this switch? He already agreed to the style you chose."

"Well, I don't know. I didn't think of that as I figure that the style of the dress for him is not as important as is the occasion and us getting married."

"Yes, of course, but don't you think that he should have a say?"

"Maybe I'll ask him. May I use your phone?"

"Of course."

Michelle walked over to the phone and dialed out. After several rings Arthur picked up.

"Hello?" Arthur said in a hurried voice.

"Hi Arthur, it is Michelle."

"Hi, is everything okay?"

"Yes, I am here at the dress shop with Jane. I am thinking about changing the style of my wedding dress and Jane suggested that I run it by you to find out what you think. I know we agreed to the ball gown style with the straps and veil; I am now thinking about switching to a more fitted, mermaid style dress, with no straps, and hair embellishments instead of a veil."

There was a pause at the other end of the phone and Michelle could hear multiple voices, some of which sounded familiar.

"Arthur?"

"Yes, I'm here. Honey, I don't know what mermaid style is, but I would prefer if we just stayed with the original style. We agreed mainly because the dress is similar to what my mother wore at her wedding. She did offer it to you for our wedding."

"I know, but this is a gorgeous style, and I would prefer something new, fresh, and unique."

"Well I wish I knew this sooner."

"This is a spontaneous thought. Besides, I didn't think it would matter to you that much since you didn't seem to care that much, nor know much about wedding dresses anyhow. Besides the fact that you liked what we picked out because it looks similar to your mom's wedding dress."

"Well, you know how close I am to my mother. Besides, it would mean a lot to her for you to be wearing a similar style. We already talked about this. I also don't have time to do any more shopping with you in person because of my work commitments. The wedding is approaching quickly, can we not just keep everything the same? I really don't have time for last minute changes."

"Alright Arthur, we will keep everything the same." Michelle could hear rustling and muddled voices in the background yet again. "Who is there with you Arthur?"

"Just work associates, you know that I interact with many at work."

"Yes. It just seems like I am hearing familiar voices."

"Well, you have met several of my work associates. That is probably why they sound familiar. Listen, I have to go. This wedding and honeymoon are not going to pay for itself. Nor is our house."

"Yes, of course Arthur." Michelle started to say that she loved him; she lost the connection from the other end of the line.

Michelle sighed, turned around, and proceeded to have her fitting with the original dress they picked out. She could not help but to feel uneasiness and disappointment of their final decision.

As Michelle was being fitted two women walked into the shop. They both seemed full of mirth, laughing, joking, floating around the shop. As Jane worked away busily at the final detailing turning Michelle around to reposition the dress, and the fabric, Michelle could not help but to overhear the women's conversation.

"I just love this colour and fabric! I cannot wait for Jonathon and I to be married," said the tall, slender woman.

Her friend replied, "Well you are one brave woman, carrying on with Jonathon the way that you are."

"What do you mean?"

"Well, despite your parents wishes, you are going to marry Jonathon anyway. That takes guts."

Gianni, the other tailor walked over to them, "Can I help you?"

The tall slender woman replied, "Yes, I have been admiring this trumpet, pure white dress for quite some time. I will take it!"

"Oh my gosh," gasped her friend, "Who is going to pay for this?!"

"Jonathan of course. Gotta start things off on the right foot. Besides he pays for everything anyway, and I obviously cannot get money from my parents."

"Did you want to try the dress on first?" asked Gianni.

"Yes, I will. How long before the dress is ready after my fitting?"

"Two to three business days at most."

"Perfect."

Gianni went to obtain her chosen dress and size. The two women waited, chatting about her upcoming wedding plans.

"What are your parents going to say about your absence?" asked the friend.

"Oh I stopped caring a long time ago," stated the tall friend.

"Aren't you worried about your family ostracizing you once they find out that you married Jonathan against their wishes?"

"It does not matter to me. They have an opinion about everything, much of which is not in my best interest. Jonathan and I have loved each other for a long time and they have never approved. My parents want to set me up with this ghastly news agent. He is nice enough, but I am not willing to hook up with and marry someone just because that is what my parents want."

The friend replied, "You are very brave, indeed. I know that you have otherwise always stuck by your family; this is one area that you and your parents have disagreed on for years. Good for you for not sacrificing your own values and happiness just to please others, even if it does mean that you may be ousted from your own family as a result."

"Yes, well you know that Jonathon and I have been in love for years. I have tried to suppress and just cannot do it anymore. He is the one I want to be with, and that is that. I know that he feels the same way about me. So on we go to elope, without a second thought."

Gianni came out with the dress and whisked the girls away to one of the fitting rooms.

Michelle stood there staring off, a feeling of sadness washed over her.

"Michelle!"

Michelle jolted in response to Jane's abrupt shrill.

"Michelle, I have been saying your name for a few minutes now. Are you alright?"

"Yes, sorry, I got lost in thought."

"Obviously," she said sternly. "I have other fittings today. Can you step down and then change? I will have the dress ready for you by tomorrow."

"Yes, sorry Jane, thank you."

Michelle could hear the girls muddled and excitable voices as she emerged from the fitting room. She looked over to see Lucy, her neighbor walking by the shop. Lucy waved, and walked into the shop. Michelle sighed to herself as Lucy was one of the biggest busybodies in the neighbourhood and she tried to avoid her whenever possible, with the exception of when her parents ask her to go visit to talk to her about subduing her gossip-tendencies, particularly at the expense of her family.

"Hi Michelle. Are you being fitted for your wedding dress?" asked Lucy.

"Yes, Lucy, actually I am just about to leave and head home."

"Well with your wedding fast approaching, no time to waste."

"Yes, I know." How did Lucy know that her wedding is fast approaching, she wondered. The two friends emerged from the fitting room and the tall one stated, "I will take this dress, as well as these hair accessories."

"You are not going to go with the matching veil?" asked Gianni.

"Oh, goodness no, I want to be flirty, thriving, unconventional, and most importantly, sexy!"

"Very well," said Gianni with a smile. We will call you when your dress is ready.

"Great, well don't toil too hard preparing it, as it won't stay on for long." The other friend laughed as they chattered non-stop upon exit from the store.

Lucy shook her head in disdain, "What sluts."

Gianni heard her and said, "Hey, I will pretend like I did not hear that."

"How is it that she comes in here, with her boyfriend's money, spending it at a whim, and has the nerve to elope despite her parent's wishes. What kind of person does that? She is clearly using him. She'll be off to her next conquest in no time. You watch, once she is bored, off she will go."

"Common, Lucy, you don't even know them. Besides, what if she really does love him? It really is none of our business," Michelle replied.

"Well she makes it her business by blabbering on the way she does, and it is not as if she is quiet about it. She is super loud and ostentatious all the way," stated Lucy disgustingly.

Michelle looked at Lucy, not responding. She often wonders how Lucy knows all that she does. It is as if she has spies out scoping the neighbourhood and reporting back to her. Or she is very observant and has eyes at the back of her head. One of the two, or both. As she is pondering this she heads for the door.

"Wait," commands Lucy. "How about we stop for tea before you head on home? You have been busy shopping, and I am sure that you could use a break."

"I don't know Lucy, I really do need to head home," says Michelle, reluctant to socialize with Lucy.

"We won't be long, I promise. Besides, it will give us time to get caught up on things."

"Fine, maybe just for an hour at most," Michelle replies and thinks to herself, yeah, and it will also give you an opportunity to dig for more dirt to spew out into the neighbourhood. Better watch what I say. Lucy followed Michelle out and they head to the local teashop.

Chapter 5: Tea With Lucy

As they walk toward the tea shop Michelle feels a knot in her stomach for she is unsure of how the conversation will go with Lucy. She is usually reluctant to socialize with Lucy because she knows that she will likely hear distorted versions of what was said later from other people. Regardless, Michelle could use a break from staying in the house caught up in her anxieties about her family and about the upcoming wedding. Michelle feels somewhat confused about why she is anxious about the wedding apart from the fact that it is a major life event. She wished that she could just let go and experience the joy of marrying a man whom she loves so much. Despite this there is a feeling of uneasiness almost like a burden placed on her shoulders. She longs for Arthur to be at her side just now so that she would have an excuse to not socialize with Lucy and yet still have an outlet to do something outside of the house for awhile.

They arrive at the tea shop, and Lucy insists on buying Michelle tea.

"It is the least you could let me do since I know I am detaining you from your usual daily activities," states Lucy.

"Well, thank you. I do appreciate it," responds Michelle.

Lucy orders and they find a seat close to a window. "Are you excited about your upcoming wedding?" asks Lucy.

"Of course, it has been a long time coming, I just wish.."

"You know, I am very surprised that you went for your fitting by yourself," Lucy interrupts, "Family support is such a crucial thing during this time in your life."

"Yes, I know. My parents mean well, but they do have lives and are otherwise occupied, and Jennifer has school. They have been there for me in other ways."

"Well, I think that it is quite selfish of your family to leave you to engage in all these activities on your own. What is more important than supporting their eldest daughter in her wedding plans? Jennifer seems to take on this mentality that your parents are demonstrating as well. She seems much more interested in chasing the boys, and her own needs in general than supporting her own sister. Good family members do not place their own individual interests first, especially not at a time like this."

"Oh, well, Lucy, in fairness to them, you do not know them well to pass that kind of judgment."

"Well, people show you who they are through their actions, much more so than through their words. Talk is cheap after all!" Lucy exclaims.

Michelle stares at Lucy for a moment, puzzled by her bluntness. Who does she thinks she is? Michelle is sure that Lucy's family is not perfect. Why doesn't Lucy just mind her own business? Michelle glances out the window in silent fuming.

"You are such a noble person, putting up with all that you do. I am sure that you are relieved that you will finally have a home of your own with Arthur in the near future."

"Right you are," Michelle agrees.

The tea arrives and they both sit in silence for a few minutes, sipping at their teas. Michelle continues to look out the window and then catches Lucy staring at her quizzically.

"Why are you looking at me like that?" Michelle asks.

"I admire your actions," states Lucy.

"Oh? How so?" Michelle asks curiously.

"You are always so calm, cool, and collected. It does not seem to matter how others are treating you or what the circumstances are, you have this grounded air about you," observes Lucy.

"Lucy, forgive me, but you really do not know me that well. You are correct that I am calm the vast majority of the time. But this is because I do not know how to behave otherwise. I need to keep focused on my upcoming wedding, and I also need to stay grounded for my family. Especially my younger sister who needs me during this time in her life when she is coming of age."

"Well, I think Jennifer will do just fine in life. She certainly has the brashness to get by. And she knows how to attract the boys, that is for sure. She will get by on her own strength, because unlike passive types, she will not allow others to trample over her. I do question the motives behind some of her actions though. Seems to me that she has a manipulative streak to her. Kind of like your parents."

Michelle looks at Lucy, again sitting in silent fuming. Who is she to babble on about her family in this way? Besides, Jennifer's motives are not her concern. As for her parent's - this unwelcome observation is so intrusive that Michelle is unsure how to respond.

"Well, I…I," Michelle stammers.

"There will come a time when Jennifer will go off on her own and you will no longer be responsible for her. Same with your parents, since you will have your own home to attend to," Lucy interrupts. Then continues, "You are so level-headed; a great quality for a wife-to-be. I do admire that quality in you, especially given all the stuff that your family dumps on you. I wouldn't take that level-headedness too far though once you and Arthur tie-the-knot. Men do need some drama and excitement to capture their attention. I think this is a quality you could learn from your younger sister, since she has no trouble capturing the attention of the opposite sex."

"Yes, well, that is high school Lucy. A man wants a woman who can be taken seriously. This is a value that I speak with Jennifer about often. Jennifer needs to learn that if she does not respect herself, nobody else will. I try to instill this in Jennifer now because life after high school, including relationships with men is very different." Michelle takes a deep breath and thinks to herself: why on earth is she talking to Lucy about this? She does not have to explain herself. And yet somehow through Lucy's comments, Michelle feels compelled to defend herself and her actions. She begins to feel this mounting frustration with herself and with the conversation.

"Did you see how our server looked at us when she brought our teas?" Lucy asks in anticipation.

"No, I did not notice."

"Really?! How could you not, she was looking at us like we had the plague."

"Like I said Lucy, I did not notice. Besides, why would she look at us like we have the plague? She doesn't even know us."

"Well, you maybe. I have seen her around. Whenever I come in here, she seems to be poking her nose where it doesn't belong."

Sounds familiar, Michelle thought to herself.

"Anyway," Lucy continues, "she probably has a lot of other people's conversations stored in that big hair of hers and is guilt-ridden as a result. No skin off my nose, I don't have anything to hide."

Lucy grabs Michelle's hand, admiring her engagement ring. "That looks like Arthur's taste. Very traditional."

Can this woman ever keep her attention on one topic for longer than a few minutes, Michelle wonders to herself.

"Well, Arthur is not that traditional, but yes in this case he is because he was influenced by his mother's rings when he made his selection," Michelle responds.

"Oh isn't that sweet. Are Arthur and his mother very close?"

"Yes, they were, when she was alive."

"Well, I would be careful about that when you two marry. You don't want someone who is treating you like their mother as opposed to their wife. Not to mention what that could do to your sex life."

"Yes, well, I am not worried about that at this stage. I know Arthur well enough to know who I am marrying."

"I sure hope so," Lucy responds.

Michelle cannot believe the nerve of this woman. She looks at Lucy with a puzzled look on her face. Lucy catches her then states,

"Oh, well, I know you are smart enough to know what you are getting yourself into. You are beautiful, smart, and have common sense. He is lucky to have you."

Michelle sits there in continued shock of this woman's abrasive tendencies and mannerisms. She is hesitant to talk to Lucy about her parent's concern; despite this she gathers her thoughts and musters up the nerve to go on. "By the way – I wanted to ask you about conversations that are apparently happening in the neighbourhood." Michelle says hesitantly.

Lucy looks at Michelle appearing intrigued "Okay, go on."

"My mother has voiced concern that you are spreading personal information about our family and she wanted me to inquire to you further about this."

"I do not spread rumours Michelle. It is just that sometimes people ask how your family is doing and it seems that you are the only reliable and dependable one in the home. It does not seem fair to you."

Michelle gazes at Lucy for a moment thinking to herself that if Lucy talks to others the ways that she did to her today that she doubts very much that Lucy has not been spreading rumours. She also seems like the type of person who would engage in regular gossip. At the very least, Michelle would not put it past her. She also seems to oscillate quite comfortably between insults and compliments. She is not sure how to take this woman, but does not have the heart to be as bold as Lucy has been. Resisting the temptation to speak otherwise Michelle replies, "I appreciate your concern but our family is just fine. You worry about your affairs just as our family worries about ours."

"Forgive me for saying so but I wish that you could apply some of that assertiveness you just demonstrated with your last statement to your own family. I do not think it is fair that others are able to carry on at your own expense. I say this to you as a friend. I do not mean to pry."

Friend? Is this woman crazy? Why would she think they are friends? Acquaintances at most, and even that is stretching it. She is not sure whether to yell or to cry. Yet Michelle knows herself and knows that she will do neither.

"Besides, who are your parents to use you to confront me?" Lucy continues, "If they have an issue with me then it is their responsibility to talk to me directly. I do not think asking you to talk to me for them is setting a good example. Quite nervy if you ask me," Lucy states in exasperation.

How nervy of this woman to say this. Michelle is too stunned to respond directly to this statement. A simple denial without elaboration about her parents virtues would have sufficed. Michelle gathers her things getting ready to leave.

"Must you go so soon?"

"Yes, I have to be getting back. Jennifer will be returning from school soon and I am anticipating a call from Arthur. Thank you for the tea."

"We should do this again soon. God only knows, you could use the social time because I know once you are married, your focus will be solely on Arthur's needs."

"Yes, well, I have my priorities straight." Michelle gets up from the table infuriated. But is masking the emotions welling up inside of her. Emotions that she tends to suppress. "I must go now – good day."

"Good day" responds Lucy.

Chapter 6: Jennifer's Return From School

Michelle returns home from her day out and is thinking about her conversation with Lucy. Why is it that Michelle can never seem to meet the approval of her peers? Lucy is very critical of Michelle's family and particularly of Michelle's choices and behaviours as a daughter and as an older sister. She never feels good enough for anyone and hopes in her heart of hearts that she will be able to meet Arthur's approval as his wife and of creating a home for them in their future life together. Michelle feels alienated in general and also lost amongst the demands of her parents, the needs of her sister and also with Arthur being away so much. Michelle makes a resolve to herself that she will continue to do all that she can to meet other people's approval. That she will persevere, and that one day through this resolve she will be truly happy as a result of this. For when others are pleased with Michelle's choices and behaviours then she too will be happy. At least she had the opportunity to make Lucy aware of her parent's concern that she gossips too much in the neighbourhood and especially about her family. Michelle is the rock in the family, she knows this, and she will not falter in her resolve to continue to be the rock. Now Michelle can report back to her parents that she has communicated the concern to Lucy, although, Michelle suspects that this will not be enough and that Lucy will continue to chatter on as she pleases. Oh well, Michelle knows that she will cross that bridge when she gets to it and especially, if Michelle's suspicion is correct then she will have more responsibility to fix the situation and make it right. At least she will be out of the house when this occurs. Michelle is making dinner for herself and Jennifer as all of these thoughts move through her mind like a mental and emotional tsunami. Michelle sighs to herself, breathing shallowly and rapidly as she prepares dinner for Jennifer and herself. Fear of the future encumbers Michelle and she aches to express this in some way. Yet she believes that expressing this fear is a sign of weakness and would circumvent her role as being a rock in this family. She must hold it together, she has to.

Michelle hears the front door open and close while she is busying herself in the kitchen. Sobs echo from the entrance way.

"Michelle!" shouts Jennifer.

Michelle rushes out of the kitchen emerging into the living room. She sees Jennifer throwing off her jacket and hurling her book bag into the room. Sobbing dramatically.

Michelle looks on in horror, "Jennifer! What is wrong?"

"Christopher is gallavanting about with Nancy again. I…I," Jennifer stammers and trails off.

"You what?"

"I don't think I am being adventurous enough for him."

"How do you mean? You are adventuruos enough for all of us."

"Well, I obviously am not for Christopher. He is always doing a u-turn back to Nancy. I cannot seem to compete with her adequately. I don't know what to do! Michelle you must tell me what to do!"

"Jennifer, I do not know what else to say. Why do you not just set your sights on someone else? He obviously has wandering eyes and you do not deserve to be treated this way."

"Michelle, I love you, but I do not think that you understand. You are always so sensible, so level, so….YOU. I am different. I need the drama, I just need Nancy to stop winning."

"Well, it is not about winning Jennifer."

"Yes it is. It is all about winning. That bitch will not get away with this. One day I will get her back, and she will get a taste of her own medicine."

"Sorry to be stating the obvious Jennifer, but she is not a good friend to you. Why don't you just walk away from the friendship. So she is popular. Being affiliated with her hurts you over and over. Is it really worth the hastle of hanging out with someone just because they are popular? Would it be the end of the world if you are not longer a part of the in crowd? At least at this point you can walk away with your dignity in tact."

"I don't care about dignity. I just want Christopher."

"This is not a healthy situation," Michelle observes.

Michelle returns to the kitchen continuing to prepare dinner. Jennifer follows Michelle and begins rummaging through the cabinets.

"What are you looking for?" asks Michelle.

"Junk food. I need as much comfort as possible." Jennifer finds a bag of pretzels in the cupboard, gets herself a cola from the fridge, places both items on the kitchen table then sits down and begins digging into the goodies.

"Try not to eat too much of that. As you can see I am preparing dinner and do not want you to spoil your appetite."

"Is my school assignment finished?" asks Jennifer.

Michelle had completely forgotten within the cyclone of her own daily activities today. Michelle does not want to tell Jennifer this though as Jennifer needs her now and she wants to be fully present for her during this time of distress.

"No, I was busy with mom and dad earlier today and then had to go for my fitting at the dress shop. I will work on your assignment tonight."

"Well, you better. It is due this week, and the last thing I need is to flunk out of school. Then Christopher will never want me. Although he would be happy as it would mean I would be more likely to focus all of my attention on him. Feeling discouraged about not doing well and school, and him becoming my focal point."

"Do not worry Jennifer, I will have it ready for you by the time it is due."

"How was your fitting at the dress shop?" asks Jennifer.

"Oh, you know, the usual. It is just one of the activities I need to do in preparation for the upcoming wedding. I ran into Lucy at the dress shop.."

"I don't know what I'll do once you leave this house," interrupts Jennifer.

"What do you mean?"

"Well, you will be gone, and I will no longer have a buffer zone between me and mom and dad."

"Oh, you'll be just fine. Besides mom and dad are always harder on me than they are on you. Before you know it you'll be on your way to moving out yourself with your future husband."

"Yes, Christopher. I have to figure out a way to recapture his attention and keep it," Jennifer grumbles in disdain.

Michelle portions their dinner onto plates, places them on the table, and sits down to join Jennifer as they begin eating.

"Is this pasta made with cream sauce?" asks Jennifer with a worried look on her face.

"Yes, it is."

"Michelle," Jennifer whines, "You know that I am trying to watch my figure. I'll be bursting out of my outfits in no time with the dinners you make. You know better."

"Yes, well I am sorry. We don't have too many choices in the fridge and pantry just now since it has been awhile since mom and dad went grocery shopping. I'll go to the market tomorrow if mom and dad are unable to." Michelle wonders in her mind if her parents will be back tonight. They are out a lot, leaving Michelle to pick up much of the slack by way of running the household. She sighs to herself as she thinks about having to do yet more errands tomorrow.

"Besides, Christopher always talks about his preference for having his women thin. I have to stay thin for him. Nancy has such a banging body. I wouldn't want to lose yet another competition with her in that department. She is on this protein and vegetable diet now. I hardly ever see her eat carbs anymore. If she gains even a couple of pounds, she is livid, and the boys are not shy about telling her that she looks like she has gained weight. Although, now she has a model figure. She could be on the cover of any magazine she wanted."

"Looks aren't everything Jennifer. You know this."

"Well, they are to me. I smiled at Christopher earlier today and the first thing that he noticed was the space I have between my two front teeth. Said that I have to get that fixed as it is way too distracting to him. He compared my teeth to Nancy's, talking about her pearly whites and how her teeth are flawless. He said that is one of the things that attracts him to her and one of the things I need to fix. Can you talk to mom and dad and convince them that I need braces? Christopher said that he doesn't want to have children that have deformed teeth."

Why is Jennifer so worried about what Christopher thinks? He sounds like such a schmuk. Besides, the teeth issue is likely genetic. Michelle has the same space between her two front teeth. Their children may very well have teeth that grow in the same way due to this genetic factor alone. What a pompous piece of work he is. Her parents have been unable, and refused to finance braces for Michelle, but she makes a note to herself to talk to them about financing this for Jennifer since this seems to mean a lot to her, as do appearances in general. Michelle looks up from her plate realizing that Jennifer is waiting for her to answer her question.

"Yes, I will talk to mom and dad."

"Thanks! You are a doll. Speaking of dolls, how does the dress look? I would have come with you but I think that the envy of seeing you prepare for your wedding would be too much to bear. Arthur is such a great guy. I wish I had a guy like that."

"Well, you seem quite taken with your own type of guy. With Christopher I mean."

"Yes, well he is my knight in shining armour no matter how fickle he may be," Jennifer replies in longing.

"The dress is fine. It is the same style. I decided to keep it the same even though I saw these two women in the shop. One of whom was trying on dresses. She tried on this gorgeous, trump style dress with no straps. She also purchased these hair excessories to go with the dress. It looked so great on her. I was looking at the very same ensemble before she came into the shop. I asked the lady who was doing my fitting if my dress could be modified to reflect some of the changes that I had admired in the items I was looking at. She was insistent on keeping the style the same as she lamented that she did not have time to make any major changes at this time. Especially with my wedding coming up so quickly. She also asked that I check with Arthur, which I did, and he was also insistent on sticking with the original style, for it reminds him of his mother's wedding dress and he has always been consumed by his mother's memory. He also said that he didn't have the time to make it to the dress shop before the wedding to approve the changes. So all in all, it went well, and the plans continue to be underway."

"When you two move in together you will be so focused on making Arthur a priority that I will take a back seat. Quite frankly, the thought of you moving out of this house frightens me," said Jennifer alarmingly.

"Why does it frighten you Jennifer? You are a very capable and willful person. You will be just fine here on your own. Besides, you are growing up so quickly. You'll blink and before you know it you too will be engaged and preparing to create a home of your own. It willl come faster than you think. You will see." Michelle said with assurance.

"I hope you are right dear sister. I just worry about standing up to mom and dad in your absence. Whenever I have a concern, you are always there to guide, to guard, and to protect. Now you will be gone, and I will feel lost. Why do you have to get married so soon? That is - before I do? It just doesn't seem fair."

"Well, there is much to be said for life experience Jennifer. If I am always the buffer between you and our parents, then you will never become proficient at facing those challenges on your own."

"You will also be so focused on Arthur," Jennifer sighed, as if she did not hear what Michelle just said. "You will be so focused on being his wife, and satisfying his needs," Jennifer continued.

"Well, I will always be here in spirit. Besides, I will just be a phone call away. I will always be there for you when you need me, you know that."

Jennifer begins to cry again, "Yes, but I always will need you. I fear that a phone call will not be enough. It is not the same as having you here physically with all of our live chats. Plus, you are the smarter one. Who will help me with my school work?" stated Jennifer with a gazing stare.

"Well you stated yourself that you do not plan on continuing your education after high school. You stated that your primary focus is on being married by the time you graduate; or at the very least in a committed relationship (too bad it may be with that schmuck Christopher, Michelle thought to herself). Before you know it, like me, your focus will be on your home and on the family you enter in to." Michelle said with conviction.

"It is easy for you to say all of these things Michelle. You do not know the struggles that I have had to endure. You met Arthur during such a crucial time in your life. You were both in high school, and Arthur is older and therefore had already established his business by the time you two became really serious. He supported your desire to attend college and so you did. Once you completed college, he had already popped the question. Throughout the duration of your relationship he has not once cheated on you. You have always been his priority, and he supports your choices and decisions. You are so lucky. I just feel like a pawn of fate, having to wrangle with keeping a man's attention let alone having him commit to me fully. Your experience is so different than mine."

"This is true and I see your point. But you are still very young. Just be patient dear sister and you will find that everything will fall into place at the right time," Michelle said compassionately.

"I already feel abandoned with you being so busy with your wedding plans," Jennifer said begrudgingly.

"Jennifer, I will never abandon you, it is just that right now my time is very divided, plus mom and dad are around less and less as we get older, leaving me responsible for the household more and more. You know I love you and would never abandon you. I just have a lot on my plate currently," Michelle replied.

"Sometimes, I feel abandoned by you, we talk and it seems like your mind and attention are elsewhere. I hear your sighs when I talk about what is going on in my life. You seem vague more often now when I need you. Sometimes it is as if you do not care," Jennifer sobbed.

"Sister, I always care.." Michelle said hesitantly.

"Now you are going off with your home and Arthur, and I will be left here all alone, with no one to talk to. With no one that understands me, and with no one that I can rely on as my source of security. This saddens me deeply."

"Jennifer, I am so sorry that you feel this way."

"Your situation and you leaving, and the way that you are distancing yourself make me feel this way," stated Jennifer rashly.

Michelle stared at Jennifer, unsure of how to respond to her statements and unsure of what to do. She felt such guilt over her sister's feelings and wished that there was something that she could say or do to make her feel better, to make her feel okay, to assure her that everything will be alright – and that everything is alright.

"Well maybe when Arthur returns, you two can talk about relationships from a male perspective. Arthur has always had such a good head on his shoulders and I am sure there is wisdom there that he can impart onto you. Especially with your current circumstances with Chistopher. For I feel that your main reason for feeling the way that you do is because of your current challenges with him and with the relationship," stated Michelle thoughtfully.

"Are you saying that I feel this way just because of Christopher?" asked Jennifer with annoyance.

"No, Jennifer, I just was thinking about your troubles with Christopher and how it may be of help to you to get a male perspective on the issue, and also because he has always had a healthy take on our relationship, with him always being so loving and committed," Michelle replied.

"Way to rub your relationship in my face Michelle. You don't need to brag about your successes so blatantly," stated Jennifer.

"That is not what I meant Jennifer, I am just trying to support you in any way that I can," Michelle responded.

"Well you can support me by not rubbing your successes in my face. I have a much more exciting high school life than you ever had. I may not be as level and sensible as you, but at least I am not ordinary. I am not afraid to put myself out there in a spontaneous manner and push the envelope when I need to. My crowd is exciting, fashionable, popular, and hip to just about everything that is worth paying attention to. This keeps me on my toes because it means that I must keep up with the trends and all things current. The way I live, no matter how unorthodox is fast-paced and exciting. There is a price to pay no matter who you choose to be," Jennifer said.

"I know, I am just trying to help any way that I can," Michelle repeated, feeling such a strong need to make her sister feel better. "I am sorry if I have made you feel anything other than happiness. My intention here is not to put you down, nor to rub anything in. I just want you to be happy," Michelle continued.

"Well I would be happiest if you were not leaving. If you could stay here for just a little while longer with me until I am ready to move out in my own prospective home," said Jennifer.

"Well you know that I am torn Jennifer. Arthur wants to get married as we orginally planned and he would not stand for deferring the wedding date any longer. We have already waited longer than he wanted. Talk with him, to get a male perspective about relationships. I think that it will help you to make better choices when it comes to men. Talk honestly with him just as you have done with me. I will let him know to prepare for having that kind of talk with you," Michelle advised.

"My choices in men are just fine. I just resent that you and Arthur are so committed when Christopher is so fickle. My choice is just fine. I know that I want Christopher. I just need to do what I can to captivate him until he no longer has the need to look at others. I must mold him into the one that I desire, through becoming all that he desires. But I will consider your suggestion to chat with Arthur about relationships to gain a male perspective," said Jennifer.

"Well it couldn't hurt," said Michelle confidently.

"Yes, maybe, just maybe I will," said Jennifer as she got up and started heading out of the kitchen. "Don't forget that my assignment is due by the end of the week. Please complete it by then," Jennifer demanded.

"Yes, of course I will Jennifer."

"Good."

After Jennifer left the room and headed upstairs, Michelle stared at the doorway for awhile thinking about the lingering effect of Jennifer's presence. She felt weighed down by guilt and shame of Jennifer's issues, especially in regard to love and relationships. She also felt really bad about her wedding approaching so quickly as this means that she will be moving out of the house soon. Michelle felt an urgency to make Jennifer feel okay in any way that she could. She just didn't know how anymore. Whenever she tried to intervene, Jennifer would counter with something else that was bothering her. Satisfying Jennifer seemed to be fewer and farther between these days. Now she will be off with a husband, and children to follow soon afterward hopefully and her attention will be even more divided. She felt a worry about being happy with Arthur in her future life especially in knowing that Jennifer is unhappy. She felt strongly that she was responsible for Jennifer and of her feelings and wished that she could do more to help her feel better. For Jennifer's pain was also her pain and she feared that this would not go away and that her attention will be taken off her future marriage as a result.

As Michelle did the washing up in the kitchen, her thoughts migrated to Jennifer's comments about bragging about her good fortune. Surely she was not bragging? Or maybe she was. Either way Michelle knew that she had to do communications better. That she had to speak to her sister in a way where she did not feel alientated and also in a way where she feels loved and supported. It hurts Michelle deeply to learn that she is making her sister feel inadequate in some way as all she is trying to do is help. Yet this intention to help seems to bite Michelle in the butt during the most inopportune moments, namely when she is trying to console and love her sister. Michelle vowed that she must do the role of being the solid rock and of being the ideal big sister better. That she would need to work on her communication skills and her ability to deliver her message in a loving way. She also made a note to herself to speak to Arthur of their conversation this night and felt that this would be good for Jennifer since Arthur is, and always has been concise and honest both in speech and in pen. Arthur is finally returning tomorrow and she can finally spend some time with the man whom she loves dearly. The man with whom she is about to marry. This should be a time of celebration, and yet it is hard for Michelle to feel this way when her sister is feeling such sadness and angst.

Michelle was so lost in her thoughts that she did not notice that she had allowed the water from the tap to fill the sink so much that it was overflowing onto the floor. In a panic, she turned the tap off and went for the mop in the broom closet, inattentive to her footing as she slipped and fell to the floor. She realized just then that the moisture she was feeling are also tears that are flowing down her face and dripping on to her arms. She had not cried in a very long time and had forgotten what this expression of emotion felt like. It has been a long time since Michelle has felt emotion so explicitly and she felt ashamed of herself that she was allowing herself to weep. She had to pull it together. She must, for her own sanity. She must for the good of her sister. She must stay strong for her. She must stay strong for this household. Michelle was so tired all of a sudden as exhaustion washed over her. She realized that she had had difficulty sleeping for weeks, and maybe even for months. She envisioned herself tossing and turning at night just as she often does in an awakened state. Restless over the series of events in her life stream. Believing that she should be something other than what she is being at the present moment. Always thinking of striving for more in her quest to perpetually do better.

Michelle mopped the water from the floor, walking into the living area and plopping herself onto the sofa. Her anticipation of Athur's return grew stronger. She needs a distraction, so she went to her study and opened up the contents of Jennifer's homework which was strewn half-hazardly by Jennifer onto her desk. Yes, a distraction, that is the answer to giving her space between her and her thoughts and emotions.

Chapter 7: Arthur's Return

Michelle fell asleep, her head nestled amongst Jennifer's homework. She had completed Jennifer's assignment for her and she knows that her sister will be pleased. Michelle knows that she will feel better when Jennifer is okay and is no longer despairing over all the things that are encumbering her at present.

"Michelle!" Jennifer calls from the bathroom.

"Yes, what is it Jennifer?" Michelle responds as she rushes toward Jennifer's screeching voice.

"Have you completed my assignment? Christopher is picking me up any minute and I need my assignment so that I can submit it today."

"Yes, I will go get it. I have finished it for you."

"Oh, thank God, I was worried that you would not have it completed on time. Hurry up, I have to go soon!"

Michelle hurriedly moves toward her study to retrieve Jennifer's assignment. She hastily moves toward Jennifer's room and finds that her room is strewn with clothes, makeup, and lingerie. Where does Jennifer get lingerie from, Michelle wonders to herself. She stands there for a moment staring at the state of her sister's room. It is never this way when they share this room, usually on the nights that they spend up all night talking.

"Michelle, hurry up! Christopher is here!" Jennifer shouts from the foyer.

Michelle runs down the stairs with her sister's assignment in tow. She reaches out to hand the assignment to her and Jennifer snatches it, already part way out the door. Michelle hears a honk from the street and gazes outside to find Christopher waiting in his car in anticipation.

"Common Jennifer, I don't have all day!" Christopher shouts. Jennifer rushes out the door, without hesitation, not looking back, and clutching on to the assignment that her sister had completed for her. She jumps into Christopher's car and he drives off, the wheels of the car squeeling against the pavement.

Michelle goes back into the house sighing to herself. Her parents remain missing in action and Michelle is left alone yet again with her thoughts. She notices that her father's appointment book is left on the coffee table. She picks it up with an uneasy feeling. For she does not like the feeling of going through other people's belongings. She begins to flip through the pages and sees a sticky note on one of the pages that reads, 'must get together with Arthur before he takes the plunge into imprisonement.' Imprisonement? What is this supposed to mean? The phone rings and Michelle walks across the room to pick it up.

"Hello?"

"Darling, I am here, in town! Will be around shortly to pick you up. I figured that we could take the afternoon and spend some time together."

"Arthur! I am so glad to hear your voice! Yes, come by, I will be waiting for you."

"Of course you will, what else do you have going but to wait for me?"

"Nothing, you are right," Michelle agrees.

"See you soon, darling."

Michelle heads upstairs and decides to pick through Jennifer's belongings including her lingerie. She decides on some sexy black undergarments and picks out a flashy bright-coloured outfit to wear. She chuckles to herself thinking, this is totally Jennifer's style. What is she doing? Peacocking? Isn't this what ostentatious males do? I guess women can ostentatiously peacock as well. She slips on the clothing feeling out of place. Feeling like this is not her. Yet she desperately wants to make a good impression with Arthur, and to captivate his attention. She then walks over to Jennifer's vanity and begins working away at applying makeup and doing her hair. What is this? She feels as if she is using her outsides as a way to feel better about what is going inside. She hesitates for a moment, feeling somewhat like a harlet. Yet she presses on, thinking that she looks somewhat like a clown. Although she is sure that Arthur will not feel the same way once he sees her. She must stand by her man, no matter how silly the sacrifice may seem to be to her. Yet the sacrifice is all that she has to hang on to just now. Without this upcoming marriage – and this relationship for that matter, Michelle believes that she would be totally lost. She cannot have that. Arthur is the only good thing she has going right now. With him, she gets the sense of feeling whole and complete. Michelle hears the doorbell ring. She goes downstairs to answer the door.

"Arthur!"

He stands at the door, holding a bouquet of red roses.

"Hi beautiful." He says with a wry smile. "Wow, these red roses match the colour of your lipstick. Since when do you wear makeup?"

"Since now," Michelle responds.

"Well, you look beautiful. You remind me just now of your sister. I always wondered when you would get her fashion sense, and also her sex appeal."

"Well, I..." Arthur interrupts Michelle, grabs her and begins kissing her passionately. Out of the corner of Michelle's eye she sees a shadow. It is Lucy walking down the street looking over at them with a searching gaze. "Come on in Arthur, it appears that we do not have privacy."

Arthur looks over and nods. He enters the house and closes the door firmly behind him.

"I am so glad that you are back, your timing is perfect! I have much to tell you," Michelle says excitedly.

"Shh, I don't think I can talk to you now the way you look. It turns me on. Let's go upstairs," Arthur says seductively.

"Wait, don't you want to catch up first? I really would love to chat and get caught up with things."

"I'd prefer to catch up while you are not talking," Arthur responds.

Arthur swoops Michelle up by her legs and whisks her upstairs. Michelle gets an uneasy feeling.

"Arthur, I was really hoping that we could save all this bedroom passion for after we are married. You know how traditional I am in my personal philosophy. Besides, I don't feel comfortable doing this in my parent's house."

"Well, your parents are not here. Common, dare to take a risk. Stop being so ordinary," Arthur eggs on.

"Arthur, I don't know, we have talked about this before."

"I know, and we have covered this ground before. What is the problem? You almost had me fooled with this sexy look you have going on here."

Michelle stops in her tracks, unsure how to respond to Arthur's comments. She will do whatever it takes to tickle his fancy. To keep his interest and his attention. She cannot afford to lose him. They resume kissing passionately, Arthur pushing Michelle into her bedroom, Michelle giving away to his pushes in a backward motion. He hurls her onto the bed. Arthur begins to slowly peel the clothing off Michelle. She feels the fabric slithering off her skin like an electric current. She feels tightness and resistance within her yet sloughs it off as she feels Arthur's kisses all over her face, neck, and chest.

"Just relax, you want me to be satisfied don't you?"

"Of course."

He enters her, thrusting slowly in a circular fashion. Arthur likes to be on top and completely in control. She breathes deeply as she feels him penetrating the walls of her vagina. She feels like a queen as she feels his manhood inside of her and their hot torsos rubbing together with such friction and passion. She forgets that she is in her parent's house as they continue to make love. She begins to moan, and Arthur begins thrusting back and forth harder and faster. He tilts her torso up whilst biting and sucking at her nipples. Suddenly he pinches at her clitoris and she heaves, moaning louder, breathing rapidly and deeply. Their torsos clapping together like a symphonic rhythm, sweating and radiating heats of passion. All of a sudden both of their bodies begin to shake and they both squeal out delightfully as they orgasm at the same time. They both gasp, catching their breath, as they lie on their backs in Michelle's bed exasperated.

"See what happens when you satisfy me? You get satisfied too," states Arthur assuredly. "Oh, I needed that." Arthur continues with a tone of satisfaction.

Michelle just smiles, nodding in agreement. Still out of breath. She feels like a queen getting a sense of being validated. Standing by her man is all there is, and all she needs. Not a bad experience of pre-marriage amorous passion, Michelle thinks to herself. For a moment, her worry about Jennifer slips away as she lies in a state of bliss.

"I want to take you out for something to eat, are you hungry?"

"Yes, you have ravaged me." They both chuckle, the bed shaking around them.

"Okay, the party is over. Let's get cleaned up and head out, we have much to talk about," Arthur commands.

Michelle gets an uneasy feeling again. The party is over, what is that supposed to mean? Michelle asks herself. She does not dare question Arthur, instead she obeys and they shower together, get dressed and head out for a meal.

At the restaurant, Arthur appears somewhat distracted.

"What is wrong?" asks Michelle.

Arthur looks over at Michelle, seemingly surprised by the question. "Oh nothing, just thinking about work, and anticipating our wedding."

"Speaking of our wedding, everything is finalized. All we need to do now is just show up for the event! Our event," Michelle states excitedly.

Arthur sighs, "Yes, I know. When are your parents coming back?"

"I'm not sure. You know my parents, they come and go as they please."

"Yes, well, that is one of the things I love about your parents."

Michelle looks at Arthur quizzically. The food arrives before Michelle gets a chance to respond. They begin eating, Arthur consuming his food ravenously. Michelle eats at a more moderate pace, looking at Arthur adoringly. Then the thought of her sister comes to mind and she is reminded to speak with Arthur about Jennifer's issues.

"Arthur, I wanted to ask you about something."

"Yes, of course. What is it?"

"It's Jennifer."

"What has she done now? That little deviant." He says smiling mischieviously.

"Well, she is having some boy trouble. She has been seeing a boy named Christopher for the past while and she is doing everything that she can to keep his interest. The problem is that he has wandering eyes and has been philandering around with other girls, namely Nancy who is supposedly one of Jennifer's closest friends."

"Well, you know men, we are the hunters, and women the nesters. Men like to spread their wings, particularly at that age. He is putting his feelers out."

"Yes, well it is at the expense of my sister's feelings. She is perpetually jealous at his advances toward other girls. I keep saying that everyone involved is so young, and that she will have more opportunities to meet other men who will treat her right."

"Well maybe he is her one and only. Who knows Michelle. She may be putting out her feelers too. You know how it is at that age, young and carefree."

"I suppose, I am just concerned that Jennifer will get hurt really badly. She has already been hurt, especially when he and Nancy started fooling around. Jennifer just seems so desperate for things to work out between them."

"Well, she has a lot of passion Michelle. At least she is reaching out and not afraid to express who she is and how she feels."

Michelle sat there somewhat puzzled. Are they just talking about Jennifer, or is he also making jabs toward her, she asks herself? Michelle decides not to vocalize this and instead to make her request known.

"Anyway, I suggested that Jennifer speak to you about relationships. I figured it would be good for her to get a male perspective, particularly from someone who has a more mature vantage point," Michelle continues.

"Of course, I will talk to her, let's go." He states abruptly. Arthur rushes the waiter for the cheque, pays, and they head back to Michelle's parents house.

Upon entering the house, they find Michelle's parents sitting sipping on drinks. "Wow, you're a site for sore eyes," states Frank, his eyes wide. Both Frank and Gail approach Arthur, hugging him heartily. Michelle stands there feeling alienated, as her parents hardly give her a second glance. She goes to speak, yet feels paralyzed and instead stands there with a simulated smile plastered across her face.

"Common Arthur," states Frank brashly, " I have some things to show you."

"Alright," Arthur replies smiling as they walk toward Frank's study.

Michelle looks over at her mother. "Has Jennifer come home yet?" asks Michelle.

"Not yet, I am sure she will be back soon. She always seems to come home at the right moment," Gail says in a vague tone.

"Well, you will be pleased to know that she continues to attend school on a regular basis. I have made sure of that," states Michelle proudly.

"Okay, good for both of you," her mother replies. She then gets up to pour herself another drink. "Do you want one of these?" Gail asks, holding a bottle of bourbon toward Michelle.

"No thanks, I don't think Arthur would be too happy with my drinking alcohol."

"Of course," Gail responds. "I guess I am drinking alone, until your father emerges from his office. From whatever it is that he and Arthur are chatting about in there."

"Yes, well you know dad. He seems to get lost in there sometimes. Whether it be by himself or with whomever he invites to join him."

"Yes, I certainly have noticed that. Are you taking care of your sister? How is she holding up?" her mother asks.

"Jennifer is doing just fine. She is having some social difficulties at school, including boy trouble. I have asked Arthur to speak with her about the latter. I figured it would be good to have some input from a mature male," Michelle explains.

"Well, whatever you think will work for her. I wish I could be here more, but you know your father: ever the hard worker and the socialite," her mother states, chuckling to herself.

"The wedding plans are finalized and am…"

"I'm going to head upstairs for a nap. Am very tired from all of the activities your father and I have been involved in over the past while," her mother interrupts.

"Yes, of course. We'll talk later."

Gail heads upstairs sluggishly. Michelle watches her longingly, wishing that she could have more heart to heart chats with her mother. She often seems like she is somewhere else. Like she is consumed with whatever it is that is going on in her head and cannot be present enough to hear what Michelle has to say about what is going on in her life. It saddens her whenever she notices this, which is often.

Arthur and her father appear in the living area with the jackets on looking like they are heading out.

"Where are you going?" asks Michelle.

"Male bonding," her father replies. "Isn't that right Arthur!?"

"Yes, we'll be back later love."

Michelle looks on disappointed. She was hoping that she would be spending some time with her hubby-to-be tonight. She feels like saying something and feels like she is seizing up again. Instead she sits there, staring at both of them.

"Not to worry, we will have plenty of time to spend together in the future, for we will soon be married," Arthur assures her.

"Yes, I know," Michelle responds meekly.

Michelle looks over at her father who nods in agreement as they head toward the door.

"See you later," her father booms.

"Yep, see you.." they are already gone before Michelle finishes her sentence.

Michelle sits alone in the room staring at the wall. She feels so alone, so alienated. She does not know what to do but press on. She must manage well, keep composed, and get it together, for everyone. She convinces herself of this. She goes upstairs and retrieves her journal, immediately beginning to write in it. She feels a sense of urgency and is unsure of where this is coming from, and so she writes. Not realizing the time, she hears the door open and close downstairs. It is late, and she hears two male voices downstairs. She heads downstairs to find her father and Arthur talking attentively to each other. They are barely aware of her presence. Her mother is sitting by the window sipping on another drink, her hands shaking.
Suddenly Jennifer walks in and everyone gets up, pleased to see her.

"Oh, divine exhaustion," states Jennifer dreamily.

"You out with the boy tonight?" asks Frank.

"Yep, how wonderful it is to have his undivided attention."

"That's my girl," states Frank proudly.

Michelle looks over at her mother who smiles meekly and walks over to give Jennifer a hug. "So great to see my beautiful daughter happy. You deserve it." Gail then retreats back to where she was sitting.

"My beautiful fiancée tells me that you are in need of some pearls of wisdom," Arthur states.

"Yes, well things are going well for Christopher and I now, but it would be great to get your input," Michelle replies.

"How about we meet tomorrow after school and we can talk?" Arthur suggests.

"Of course. I'm going to bed now. See you later."

Michelle decides to follow her sister upstairs. She is tired also, and is looking forward to spending the day with Arthur tomorrow. As she begins to fall asleep, she hears the faint voices of her parents bidding Arthur farewell. Finally they are wrapping things up down there. She looks at the clock and it is almost 3 am. Time seems to go by so fast when she is dwelling in her thoughts. She wonders what they have to talk about for so long and yet does not worry as she knows that she will have Arthur all to herself tomorrow and finally he and Jennifer will have the chance to talk as well.

Michelle wakes up to hear voices downstairs again. She showers and heads downstairs to join whoever is there. Her father and Arthur are talking in the kitchen.

"Is Jennifer at school?" asks Michelle.

"Yes, she went off with Christopher this morning," says Arthur.

"What about mom?" asks Michelle.

"She is out running some errands, and then we are going to meet up later with some business associates. You should get out more Michelle, treat yourself, do something fun. Your whole life is not about this upcoming wedding you know," Frank suggests.

"I know, but it is prevalent in my mind as it is fast approaching," Michelle replies.

"Arthur and I are heading to my office for the day. I figured I would show him the ropes, maybe play some squash."

Michelle looks surprisingly at Arthur, "I thought we were going to spend the day together."

"Yes, darling, I know. It is just that your father and I figured that he would show me what he does at work. I have been thinking about a possible career change and this is an opportunity for me to get an inside view of his work life," Arthur replies.

"I did not realize that you were thinking about a career change. You seemed happy where you are now," Michelle says with confusion.

"Yes, well things change Michelle. It may even be a bigger salary. After all, I have to provide for you and – eventually – our growing family. Someone has to put food on the table. With the upcoming wedding and our honeymoon afterward, this seems like the perfect time to become acquainted with your father's work."

"Well, I was really looking forward to spending time with you today."

"We will have plenty of time together. In the meantime, I have much to do, including meeting up with your sister this evening. I will give you a call later," Arthur assures.

"Okay," Michelle states disappointingly.

"See you later."

"See you later."

Michelle stands there, puzzled. Now what? She had planned her whole day around spending time with Arthur. Now what was she going to do with herself? She decides that she will freshen up and treat herself to a movie. At the theatre she sits there, absorbing none of the film. She resents that her father is monopolizing Arthur's time. He seems to be getting in the way of what she wants to do, and how she would like to spend her time. Now Arthur will go from his office to pick up Jennifer and this means that she will have even less time to spend with him today. It is not fair. Maybe she will join Jennifer and Arthur this evening. She decides to take a walk to Jennifer's school and surprise her with this. As she is walking she sees Lucy walking in the opposite direction. She starts to step off the curb with the intention of walking on the other side of the street, in the hope that she will not have to speak with Lucy. It is too late. Lucy is quickly approaching her, calling out her name.

"Michelle, wait up!" yells Lucy.

Michelle stops in her tracks and waits, greeting Lucy as she approaches.

"I saw your sister earlier today during her lunch hour. She really seemed quite upset."

"Why? What happened? Did you speak with her?" Michelle asks alarmingly.

"Yes, I spoke with her briefly. She was quite distraught about her boyfriend. Apparently they are having trouble again."

Why can't Lucy just mind her own business, Michelle thought to herself. She is such a meddler. "Yes, well, relationships can have their ups and downs. I have faith that things will work out for the best for my sister. Now if you will excuse me."

"Where are you going?" asks Lucy.

Why does she ask such things? It is none of her business where I am going, Michelle thinks to herself.

"I was actually heading to the school to surprise my sister. Now that you mention that she is upset, it is all the more reason to head over there and provide my support," Michelle replies.

"I think that Jennifer has made plans of her own," Lucy replies.

"What do you mean? School isn't out yet," Michelle states, feeling confused.

"I saw Arthur come around to pick her up, it looked like they were heading somewhere."

"I know, we had arranged for my fiancée and Jennifer to meet this evening for a meal and a chat, to provide further support."

"And you are okay with that?" Lucy asks suspiciously.

"Of course, it was my idea and Arthur agreed. We both only want the best for Jennifer."

"Well, I would be wary of that girl spending time with your fiancee," Lucy warns. "She seems to be quite fickle where the opposite sex is concerned and I don't know if I would trust any man with her. Particularly with the man I am about to marry."

"Yes, well I trust Arthur."

"Good for you, that you have that kind of relationship with Arthur. Listen, I was thinking of having some people over for lunch tomorrow. You are more than welcome to attend, and maybe bring your family along. I spoke with Jennifer about it too."

"Okay Lucy, maybe we will. I must be going now. Goodbye."

"Bye," Lucy responded.

Michelle continued to walk toward Jennifer's school. She walked by a restaurant proximal to Jennifer's school and heard that they make great desserts on site. She decided to head in and pick something up for later and surprise everyone. As she walked in, she spotted Jennifer and Arthur sitting across the room talking. There was laughter, and there appeared to be intense conversation.

"Can I help you?" asked a waiter from behind.

Michelle spun around to see a cheerful face. "I was just going to go over to the dessert section to pick up a few items. Can I use your washroom first?"

"Yes, the washrooms are just over there," the waiter said and pointed.

"Great, thank you," replied Michelle.

Michelle walked slowly toward the washroom and hid herself behind one of the pillars. She was glad that Arthur and Jennifer had not spotted her. She was unsure why she was hiding, for she trusts her fiancée, and yet there was this uneasy feeling. They were speaking intently to each other and Arthur reached out and touched Jennifer's shoulder. She smiled and was nodding, apparently taken by whatever it was that he was saying to her. He stroked her cheek and then took her hand. She responded by taking his hand in return. Well, Arthur is very affectionate and warm, Michelle told herself. It is natural that Jennifer would be so comfortable with him. She was surprised that they were meeting so early. She supposes it is because Jennifer was just too upset to finish her school day today. Michelle could certainly appreciate this, as there have been plenty of times that Jennifer has left school early, distraught, seeking comfort from her big sister. Nothing to be worried about. She was so consumed with watching them, trying to assess the situation, and analyzing, that she did not realize she was moving toward the exit toward the back of the restaurant. Because she was backing away, she did not see that there was a waiter heading in the opposite direction behind her. She bumped into him, jolted back into her body.

"Oh, so sorry, I was not paying attention," Michelle said. Turns out it was the same waiter who greeted her when she arrived at the restaurant.

"No worries. How about those desserts?"

"You know, I think I have changed my mind on that. Maybe some other time."

"Sure, okay. Thank you for stopping in. Come again."

Chapter 8: Lunch with Lucy

     Michelle had a fitful sleep that night. She resented that her fiancée was out and about, seemingly having a good time with her sister, and father and not with her. She figured that all would be well once she had a partner and all the future prospects that go along with it: the sharing, the caring, the love. She had pined for this vision since she was a little girl. Finally, this prospect is becoming a reality, an escape from this feeling of emptiness she has experienced all of her life, yet this feeling of emptiness had returned to her. Currently, this feeling is stronger than ever, eating away at her like a cancer, slow, gradual, and painful. This did not seem fair. She feels that she is always there for others, yet when the time came when she needed someone, nobody returned the favour in kind. She felt alienated and ostracized, and yet her life is a good one. There was nothing that she could think of that was fundamentally wrong with her life. She tossed and turned with these persistent, and negative thoughts. It was like a bombardment of torment from which she could only get temporary relief. She had a sickening feeling in the pit of her stomach that this radio of negative thoughts would not leave her. That she would have to deal with these thoughts for the rest of her life. She feared greatly that her internal protestations would become a physical reality, and this terrified her. Yet she had no one that she felt that she could express this to. Arthur needed her to be a good partner. He always said that it is paramount that a woman stand by her man. She needed to be there for Arthur and to hold it together. To hold it together for everyone. She tossed and turned until finally falling asleep, hearing giggles and muddled voices echoing from downstairs, the noise bombarding around her room, augmenting her feelings of resentment as she dozed off to sleep.

     Michelle woke up and the house was totally silent. She rolled over and craned her neck to see what time it is. Oh my goodness, it is 11 am! Michelle could not remember the last time she had woke up this late in the morning. Why did no one wake her? She fleed to the washroom moving swiftly in and out of the shower and then proceeded to rummage through her belongings with the intent of getting ready for the lunch that Lucy is hosting in her home. She moved swiftly down the stairs and found a note nestled behind a magnet on the fridge in the kitchen. She snatched it feeling a sense of irritation wash over her. She was not feeling so fresh now as she anticipated reading the contents in the note. Arthur's note read:

Dear Michelle:

'Went out with your father this morning. Have dropped Jennifer off at school. Not sure where your mom is, said she would return at some point later today. See you soon, Arthur.'

It was the day before Michelle and Arthur's wedding and she felt this haunting quality in the house. Despite the fact that no one was around, Michelle was grateful to have this time alone as she knew that spending time at Lucy's place would be enough for her to handle for one day. She began to feel excited again about starting out fresh with Arthur. A new beginning, one where there is a chance that she will feel – unlike how her parents make her feel – which is adequate and in sync with her surroundings. Finally a chance to start again. Look at the time, almost noon, time to head over to Lucy's and go at this lunch alone. Unlike Arthur, Michelle had no excuse for not attending, so off she goes.

As Michelle approaches Lucy's entrance way she felt this desire to turn around and go home. This feeling was augmented by the sound of laughter radiating out into the street like an orchestration. Despite Lucy being a busybody, she sure did have a lot of friends. Her home environment was usually quite invigorating and mirthful. Michelle felt overwhelmed by anxiety, feeling separate from her body, so much so that she was not aware that she had already rang the door bell. Just as soon as she was turning around to leave, the door flew open and Lucy filled the door with her presence. The smell of lilacs and lavender saturated Michelle's olfactory sense and she knew that there was no turning back now.

"Michelle! So glad that you could make it," stated Lucy excitedly. She reached out and embraced Michelle with a hug, and for a brief moment, Michelle felt relieved.

"Come on in and make yourself at home. We have finger foods prepared. Let me take your coat."

Michelle allowed Lucy to take her coat as she felt the fabric slither off of her trunk and arms. Michelle entered the living area to find several of Lucy's friends, some of which were neighbours socializing and chatting away.

"Would you like something to drink?" Lucy asked.

"Sure, I'll have a sparkling water," Michelle replied.

"No wine for you Michelle? Come on, let your hair down and join us for an early happy hour."

"Oh, I don't know. Arthur said that he doesn't like it when I consume alcohol. Especially during the day. I.."

"Well Arthur is not here to order you around now is he? Common, it is the day before your wedding and you are among friends. Loosen up, there are no judges here, only supporters," Lucy said wryly with a smile.

Michelle hesitated, "Okay," she stated apprehensively.

"Oh good, I knew somewhere underneath there I would find a brave woman," stated Lucy with assurance.

Michelle looked toward the h'or deovres and decided to walk over to one of the tables to obtain one. She went for a few crackers with cream cheese and lox placed on top, some mini meatballs, as well as some fruit with a decadent looking dip. Lucy came up from behind with a glass filled with red wine.

"Thank you. You remembered that I prefer red to white."

"How could I forget?" stated Lucy mischieviously.

"Come on, join us for a chat. Lunch should not be very long if that husband-to-be of mine doesn't know what is good for him," Lucy said with a wink.

Lucy grabbed Michelle's arm and directed her toward a few women seated in an alcove surrounded by windows. The light was pouring in filling the alcove with warmth providing a welcoming environment that Michelle was drawn to immediately. Michelle sat in one of the plush chairs admiring Lucy's plants and became attentive to the conversation.

"Hi Michelle, long time no see. This is my friend Lois."

"Hi Linda, nice to see you again. And nice to meet you Lois."

"You too," stated Lois.

"You have met Angela have you not?" Lucy asked.

"Ah yes, of course. Nice to see you again too."

"And you," replied Angela.

Lucy's fiancée – Michael – walked into the alcove informing the ladies that lunch would be in approximately half an hour.

"Thank you darling," said Lucy adoringly.

"I also have everything all set up for you and I this evening; we can talk more about this later," Michael continued.

"Wonderful. You will pick my sister and her family up from the airport, right?" asked Lucy.

"Yes, of course," Michael stated.

"Great, as you know how I feel whenever they visit. Filled with anticipation and glee. Maybe we will follow suit with a growing family of our own in the near future. I know this is always inspired in me whenever I see her, the lucky woman that she is," Lucy pondered.

"Well as gorgeous as you are, we shouldn't have any problems," Michael replied as he embraced Lucy adoringly and gave her several kisses on the mouth.

"Oh Michael, you are too much. We have guests! Save this for later," Lucy said, as she giggled.

"Oh I will, gorgeous!" Michael said.

"Get a room you too!" Lois said jokingly.

Michael let go of his embrace and returned to the kitchen to get lunch ready for their guests.

"You two are so lucky. Such a stark difference from your previous relationship. And not only that, you two are engaged! Goes to show that all that fuss and pickiness has paid off. You appear to have your dream relationship," said Linda supportingly.

"Oh yes, I know. I just found that I had to work on myself before taking the plunge into another relationship. Now that I respect and value myself, I have drawn the right partner to me." Lucy reflected.

"Well you are very fortunate. Congratulations," Angela said.

"I will see your sister tomorrow at the wedding. It has been awhile. It will be nice to see her and her family there," Michelle stated.

"Yes, the whole clan of us will be there," said Lucy. "By the way, how is Arthur these days? How come he has not joined us here today?" Lucy continued.

"Well, he has been spending a lot of time with my father. I have also asked him to spend some time with Jennifer so that he can impart some of his wisdom regarding relationships from a more mature, male perspective," Michelle explained.

"I don't know if I would tolerate my partner spending time with everyone else other than me especially right before we are about to be married," Lucy said.

"I know, but Arthur is marrying into the family. He just wants to make a good impression," Michelle defended.

"Well, I can appreciate this where your parents are concerned. I just think that Jennifer is a big girl. There is no reason why she cannot work some of these issues out herself. That is one of the reasons I did not invite her to join us. Besides monopolizing your time, she appears very needy. I often feel bogged down just watching you two interact," Lucy said honestly.

"Well, I did ask Arthur specifically to speak with her. I just feel this is my responsibility," Michelle said.

"You mean Jennifer is your responsibility?" Angela asked curiously.

"Yes," Michelle stated abruptly.

"Michelle, do not be ridiculous. I am not judging you, but may I speak honestly with you?" Lucy asks.

"Of course," replies Michelle.

"My sister and I had a relationship similar to what you are describing with Jennifer. She would often bog me down with her issues and I found that my life was no longer my own. All of a sudden one day I turned around and my life became all about her issues and needs. This was at the expense of my own peace of mind. One day, I said to myself – enough! I am not responsible for her, and I will no longer allow her to make me feel as if I should be. Now mind you, it helps that we no longer live in the same city, and that she now has a family of her own. But I really had to put my foot down to lay down some boundaries, and our relationship is much healthier as a result. Sure we still have our tiffs; however, things are much improved as I firmed up and discovered a new found freedom as a result. Just something to think about," Lucy says.

Michelle sat there, stunned at Lucy's self-assurance. She took a sip of wine and replied, "Yes, well she is my little sister and I strive to look out for her."

"Of course, but try not to over extend this at your own expense," Lucy advised.

"I can really relate to this conversation in my own way," stated Linda thoughtfully.

"How do you mean?" asked Lucy.

"Well, my sister – who is older – is always so interested in my life. She is often providing advice, and can be quite over-protective by nature. That is probably one of the reasons why she is such a successful business woman. Very detail oriented, and precise in her approach to things. Anyway, her last partner had left her because he found her to be too controlling. It didn't seem to matter how good-natured her efforts were – it was too much for him to deal with as he had the impression that she was always meddling in every single detail of his life. Now we live in different cities too, and whenever I see her, I understand better why she is a single woman now. Now I say this because she very much fancies to be in a relationship, as long as she is treating her partner like a younger sibling, I fear that her desire will not be realized. For this approach works great when you are running a business, for in that environment, is an expectation that she take control. Maybe this desire for control is the reason for her love of animals; she won't get any protestations from her lovely pets as she strives to run the show!" Linda said.

The other women laughed at this last statement.

"She will have a full-blown zoo at the rate she is going!" Lucy said jokingly.

"Yeah, tell me about it," replied Linda.

"Well, my parents would lose it if I stopped looking after Jennifer. Besides, I am so used to being the rock. The level-headed one. The one who looks out for everyone. How could I give this up after all of this time? I fear what may be around the corner for me if I gave up that familiarity. Besides, I am soon to be a married woman, so what does this all matter anyway? Things are about to change in my life and in my surroundings," Michelle replied.

"Lunch is ready!" Michael shouted from the dining area.
The women scooped up their glasses of wine and headed toward the dining area.

"Remember to take care of you. We can talk anytime if you need to," Lucy whispered.

"Sure," replied Michelle, feeling confounded by the conversation they all just had.

As they sat and ate the wonderful lunch that Michael had prepared, Michelle looked on at the affection that Michael and Lucy displayed toward each other.

"So what are your plans, once your sister arrives Lucy?" Angela asked.

"Well, we are attending Michelle's wedding tomorrow of course. Then, my sister will be helping me to get my floral business up and running. Michael and I have been working hard to make this vision a reality and despite Michael's really hectic schedule, he has been such a wonderful support to me in this endeavor," Lucy responded.

"I am surprised that you are pursuing this Lucy. You don't have to work after all. Michael provides for you well," stated Angela.

"Yes, well, I don't believe in having a man provide for me. Why should I live up to any expectations other than my own? I am passionate about opening up my floral business. This has been a vision that I have had for a long time," Lucy replied.

"This is one of the things that attracts me to Lucy," Michael stated lovingly, "She goes after what she wants. Moreover, she has a desire to go after her dreams and to make them a reality, regardless of whether or not she has a partner. She is independent like I am, and we make a choice to be together with this mutual understanding. We are on the same wavelength," Michael continued. They both leaned in toward each other kissing briefly, he reaching out, looking into her eyes and stroking her face. They both resumed eating.

"I admire your fearlessness Lucy. You are an inspiration," said Linda excitedly.

Michelle sat back, observing everyone around the table and listening to the conversation intently. There was something deep inside of her that resonated to this discussion, yet it sickened her at the same time. She felt plagued by envy as she sat there seeing how well Michael and Lucy connect and how they parallel each other's desires and values. This type of dynamic she was witnessing between Michael and Lucy is one for which she is unfamiliar. She is also unfamiliar with the self-assuredness that Lucy was displaying. She found herself feeling very uncomfortable with observing this. Almost like this is something that she should not be witnessing, nor should be apart of. Why couldn't she just feel like she measures up? Why was she all of a sudden feeling inadequate in all of her efforts? Where was this feeling coming from? Suddenly she felt animosity as she believed that she should not be feeling this way. It is not right, and so she resumed denying her feelings and returning to the level-headed woman that she is comfortable being, whilst surpressing her feelings.

Everyone continued to eat, to laugh, to converse, and Michelle was sure that she was apart of this interaction with everyone, and yet at the same time felt apart from everyone. She talked, seemingly robotically, absorbing no more of the conversation around the table after Lucy's announcement of pursuing her own business with Michael's support. After all was said and done, and Michelle felt uncomfortable enough to want out, she made her excuses.

"Lucy and Michael, thank you so much for hosting this lunch. Everything was delicious. I must go now, and rest up for tomorrow," Michelle said distantly.

"Yes of course," Michael and Lucy said in unison. "Let me see you out," Lucy continued.

Michelle stood up, bidding everyone farewell, and followed Lucy to the doorway.

"So glad that you could join us," Lucy said. "We should do this more often."

"Yes, I know, and thank you. Will see you tomorrow. Have a good evening with your sister and family," Michelle replied.

"We will, thank you. Know that all is not lost once you tie the knot. Relationships that are built on relying on others for our happiness are not built to last," Lucy said.

"Yes well, we all have our ways of bringing happiness into our lives. I like to think that I have a say as to how this occurs in my life. Goodnight." Michelle said as she walked out the door.

"Goodnight Michelle."

Michelle's head was filled with thoughts of resentment and envy. She wished that she was as self-assured as Lucy is. They carry on, seemingly without a care in the world, and they allow each other to feel this way. How is it that Michelle cannot replicate this with Arthur? She is always so on guard, so focused on behaving herself, and so focused on being the rock with everyone and everything, and holding everything together. She felt inadequate. A feeling triggered by her comparison to Lucy and Lucy's situation. Michelle sighed to herself, suddenly feeling overwhelmed by tomorrow's wedding. She felt too tired to do anything other than go straight to bed. So she did, whizzing by her family who barely noticed her come in, she retired until morning.

Chapter 9: The Wedding

Michelle's wedding day was bright and sunny. She had woken up to the sound of bird's chirping outside of her window, and she was glad that it was a new day. All of the negative feelings she was experiencing the day before at Lucy's were a distant memory and she was happy to get on with things and to get on with her new life with Arthur. She had been looking forward to this day since she was a little girl and it was finally coming to fruition. Suddenly, her thoughts and feelings were filled with prospects and possibilities as she finally was about to escape the encumbered existence that she has experienced at her parent's house and with her sister for all of her life.

Her bridesmaids, friends, and family surrounded her as she was assisted with the final touches of smoothing out her ensemble of wedding dress, veil, hair pins, and jewelry. She was also being assisted with applying the final touches of makeup before walking down the aisle. The buzz of conversation surrounding her was an effusive expression of how beautiful she looked, how excited others are for her, and congratulatory statements.

Suddenly, Michelle was being ushered toward the main hall. It was time! She was finally doing this!

The music began to play, and all rose, turning around, looking on at Michelle in admiration and excitement. Michelle gazed at Arthur who was standing at the altar awaiting her to join him as she embarked on her long walk down the aisle. The room smelled of florals, perfume, and talc powder. Her walk seemed to go on forever, for she could not wait to join her soon-to-be husband and finally get this over with. For she knows that once this deal is done, there will be no turning back. She will be completely his, and he will be completely hers. This marriage would change them both for the better, and she feels that this wedding, and all the attention she is garnering with it, is validating her perspective. Finally, she would be free. Finally, her dream is becoming a realization.

Her father handed her hand over to Arthur's and Michelle could feel Jennifer's presence (her maid of honour) right behind her.

Maybe now that Jennifer is witnessing this sacred union, she will be inspired to seek out a loving partner of her own, someone who treats her with respect, something parallel to what she and Arthur demonstrate and symbolize through their choice to wed this day. Oh how Michelle wishes this for her sister.

Arthur and Michelle proceed to exchange their vows. When they finish exchanging vows, Arthur kisses her sweetly and as they put their rings on each other, Michelle feels like a queen. Finally totally present with Arthur, all eyes on both of them, she feels that they both have arrived, engaging with each other completely, even if only a few words are exchanged, which is the case.

After the wedding ceremony, the two sit at the front of the reception room where kind words and announcements are exchanged. Michelle presents Arthur with a speech:

"Arthur, my love. I knew from day one that there was a connection. You and I together, in a state of union. Enjoying each day to the fullest. You are the one for me, and now we have made it official. I will spend the rest of my live striving to make you happy through thick and thin. I love you sweetie!" Michelle stated as they embraced, kissing passionately.

Applause from the onlookers.
Arthur presents Michelle with a speech:

"Michelle, I've tried to tell you in many ways how I think that I feel. None could be a greater expression than Yeats, so I will read this to you: Love is all unsatisfied.."Arthur proceeded to read Music for Words Perhaps, by William Butler Yeats. Michelle knows that Arthur is a Yeats fan; however, she is unsure why he chose one of these diatribes at their wedding? The only parts she remembers are when he read "scoff and lour.." and "all could be known and shown if time were but gone." Michelle feels stunned at how much this last statement resonates with her. She catches a few glimpses who are mirroring the scowl on her face, and immediately begins to smile. She does not want to put a damper on her wedding day through explicit expression of being confounded. So she puts on her smiley mask and it stays pasted on for the remainder of the reception.

Now it is time for Michelle's father to say something, and he proceeds to do so, taking the microphone out of Arthur's hand, immediately followed by a handshake.

"My daughter, finally married off. What can I say, she is a good sport, with a good heart. I can be very demanding and she has always heeded to that. This reaction to my tendencies has elicited a respect for her that I am sure will be matched when she demonstrates who she is being as a wife." He looks over at Michelle, chuckling. "Congratulations kiddo," he walks over, giving her a hearty hug.

Now it is Jennifer's turn, "Dear sister, you have gotten me out of more scrapes than I care to admit. You are a great big sister, and I will miss our late night chats, and having ready access to you living under the same roof! Although, I can just come over and visit and receive your moral support anytime! I don't know what I would do without you, for it is as if I wouldn't be able to get through life without your guidance and direction. Congratulations big sister!" They embraced, with their eyes filled with tears.

Her mother took her turn at the microphone, briefly stating, "Just as I had hoped, my eldest is getting married first. If you are anything like I am, then you will be great. Like me, you have such a kind, nurturing, and caring nature. I have raised you well to fulfill this role. Congratulations sweetheart." They embraced.

Now it is time for the couple to have their first dance and they do, they break ground on the dance floor and have their first dance as a married couple.

The rest of the night is a whirlwind of activities as everyone approaches the couple chattering away, with lots of smiles and lots of cheer. Michelle weaves through the crowd, dancing with many along the way. She decides to head out to the patio, where the reception has spilled out onto. She jokes and laughs with the children toying with the balloons, confetti, and streamers outside. Michelle goes for some punch, and turns around to find Lucy standing behind her.

"Great wedding. You could not have picked a better day, and this night is beautiful, nothing but indigo skys and sparkling stars," Lucy stated. "It was a little strange don't you think? The poem that Arthur chose I mean," Lucy continued.

"Well, you know Arthur, he can be quirky at times. It is one of the things that made me fall in love with him," Michelle replied.

"Yes, I suppose that makes sense," stated Lucy.

"Say, Lucy, have you seen my sister? I haven't seen her since the beginning of the reception," Michelle inquires.

"She slipped out awhile ago, I think she said that she needed some air and that she was going to walk through the gardens for awhile. By the way, I noticed that Christopher did not come. Is everything okay between those two, or are they on the rocks again?" asked Lucy.

"I don't know Lucy, it is on again, off again. I find it hard to keep up, plus I am so consumed with the wedding and our honeymoon, that I have not given it much thought just now," Michelle replied.

"Yes, well consuming oneself with many activities at once can be a great form of escapism," Lucy said under her breath.

"What did you say?" asked Michelle.

"Oh nothing, you know me, I can ramble on sometimes," replied Lucy.

"Yes, well, if you'll excuse me, I am going to go and search for my husband," Michelle stated then rushed off.

"See you later," Lucy called after her.

Michelle began her venture through the gardens. There were bursts of colour displayed by all the beautiful plants and flowers that were reflecting the moonlight. There were also dark shadows sandwiched in between the motley clusters. In one such shadow, Michelle tripped on a rock, losing her balance, and descending toward the ground. She reached in front of her to catch her fall. Feeling rattled, she suddenly heard whispers not too far off into the distance. She gathered her dress and slowly began to rise. There was a gazebo off in the distance and she spotted Arthur and Jennifer through the trellis. They were sitting on a wooden bench seemingly engrossed in deep conversation. Michelle had an uneasy feeling and her stomach felt like it did a flip-flop before she proceeded to make her presence known to them both. As she walked over, Arthur reached out and began to stroke Jennifer's hair. As she approached, Michelle was close enough to overhear their conversation.

"You are so beautiful Jennifer. Beautiful beyond measure. I know you feel despair now because of Christopher's treatment of you. Like things will not get any better. They will, and one day you will have a beautiful relationship," Arthur assured Jennifer.

Jennifer looked into Arthur's eyes. "You are terrific. My sister is a lucky woman."

"Yes, well I hope she feels the same way you do," Arthur said playfully.

"Well she is crazy if she doesn't," Lucy giggled flirtatiously.

Michelle cleared her throat, making her presence known. Both Jennifer and Arthur looked up, both with self-conscious expressions on their face.

"Sweetheart," said Arthur, "I was just providing your sister with more of my pearls of wisdom."

"Yes, well, I have been looking all over for you. Have you been out here for long?" Michelle inquired.

"Long enough," Arthur replied. He looked over at Jennifer, "We can continue this conversation anytime you want. We hope to see you around our home regularly."

"Well, not too regularly I hope. Jennifer will be busy with her own life, I am sure," Michelle stated.

"Are you saying that you don't want me around regularly once you make the big move?" Jennifer asked.

"Not at all. You know what I mean. You are quite the socialite so I would not be surprised if your visits are few and far between, given your track record," Michelle replied.

"Given my track record I'll be hanging off your home life, how could I not?" Jennifer said.

I hope not, Michelle thought to herself. She really does long for quality time with Arthur free of interruption. Besides, Michelle feels threatened, especially after witnessing this last encounter between them, although she will not dare admit this to either one of them.

"Yes, well there will be no hanging off anyone just now. Arthur and I must get ready for our honeymoon. We have a plane to catch." Michelle took Arthur's arm, clutching on to his sleeve. Arthur kissed Jennifer on the cheek and as Michelle watched, she shuddered.
Despite this, she gave her sister a hug, and bid her farewell.

Michelle and Arthur walked through the reception venue, hugging many. It was time for Michelle to throw the bouquet, and not surprisingly, her sister caught it, and with such passion.

Michelle looked over and winked at her sister. They got into the vehicle, surrounded by a shower of sparkled, confetti, and flower pettles as their guests threw them up into space, and gravity took effect drawing the matter down all around them. Michelle waved adamantly at her parents, who stood toward the front of the crowd alongside her sister. As the car pulled off, Jennifer ran after it exclaiming, "Goodbye, have a wonderful honeymoon, I love youuu."

Chapter 10: The Honeymoon

Arthur had always wanted to go to the Carolinas for a vacation, and so this is where they decided to have their honeymoon. They stayed in a nice cozy hotel right on the shores of Myrtle Beach. On the first day, they spent time lounging on the beach taking in the blue skies, pearly sand, and the beautiful aquamarine ocean. Finally she had an opportunity for some quality time to spend with Arthur. He was always so busy working, and when visiting with her parents, spending time with her father, that she really appreciated having some alone time with him. Free of schedules, agendas, other people's demands and interferences.

At this moment, they are walking hand in hand along the shoreline.

"Do you think that we could just stay here forever? Just forget about our lives back home, and just be here, you and me, always together, all the time?" Michelle stated dreamily.

"Yes, that would be nice. You know that is not possible though silly. After all, I have to put food on the table. I also think, after awhile I would get bored," Arthur replied.

"Bored? Being here with me?"

"No, of course not. I just mean that I am a go-getter. I go after what I want. I like to be busy doing things," Arthur clarified.

"Yes, well one can dream."

"Yes, and you do that very well," said Arthur.

Arthur reached down and picked up two seashells. "This represents the two of us. Connected in love, connected naturally, washed up by the sea. They symbolize the fact that we have come together through a random sequence of events, and joined in union through the chaos," Arthur reflected.

"Chaos? I hardly think so. We are so meant to be together. I will make you so happy," Michelle said gazing up at him.

"Yes, well, I don't believe that anything happens in an orderly fashion. We collided, we are married, and now here we are," Arthur said distantly.

This last statement bothered Michelle. Why could he not see things the way that she does? She felt that he was ruining the moment for her, and often feels this way whenever they interact this closely. Not wanting to ruin the moment for him she remains silent. Taking a deep breath, oxygenating herself with the surrounding sea air. There is a DJ on the beach playing music.

"Let's dance," commanded Arthur.

"Okay," Michelle obeyed.

Arthur drew Michelle into his arms and they danced slowly on the beach, the shore washing up over their feet. Their bodies moved with the rhythm of the music and also with the pulsating rhythm of the waves. They danced in silence for a few minutes, Michelle losing herself in Arthur's arms.

"Do you want to eat out tonight? The menu at our hotel is not appealing to me, and I would like to see what they have to offer in town," Arthur said.

"Sure, Arthur. Whatever you want to do, I want to do."

Arthur smiled sheepishly, kissing her lightly on the mouth.

"Let's go, I'm starting to feel hungry," Arthur said.

"Already? I wouldn't mind staying here for a little while longer," Michelle stated.

"Well you don't want your man to starve do you? Besides, you may not feel hungry now but by the time we get into town, I'm sure you will be," Arthur said.

"Yes, I'm sure you're right. Well, if we must, let us go," Michelle replied.

They walked slowly toward the stretch of hotels. Arthur was feeling rather frisky when they returned to their hotel room. He wanted Michelle at that moment. His amorous advances made Michelle feel like a queen, and they made love passionately. Afterward, they both threw their sweaty bodies backward on to the linens.

"Arthur, can't we just order in? I am exhausted, and would not mind making this a nice quiet evening in," Michelle requested.

"Michelle, you know me. I am not one to stay in. We are in South Carolina! Let's paint the town red and check things out!" Arthur exclaimed.

"Okay," Michelle said hesitantly.

"I need more energy from you. Where is your fire? Your spirit? This is an exciting time for us!" Arthur exclaimed.

"Yes, I know. I'm sorry. I will do better," Michelle said.

"Well you don't need to do better, just show more enthusiasm. You know that I can't stand a flat affect," Arthur replied.

They both freshened up and headed into town. Arthur chose a restaurant with all-American fare, that also had a casino affiliated with it. The waiter showed them to their table, and Arthur ordered for both of them.

"Ribs? Arthur, you know that I am not a big fan of red meat."

"What are you going to have? Seafood? Fish tastes fishy. How can you stand eating that?" Arthur stated.

"Can you just let me order for myself for a change?"

"Not at this table. I think the smell of seafood would spoil my appetite. You'll have to indulge in your seafood on your own sweetheart," Arthur said.

"Fine, I'll stomach your red meat for one night."

"You will have to stomach it for more than just one night, since you'll be doing all of the cooking," Arthur said with a wink.

"Yes, I guess you are right," replied Michelle.

"How was lunch at Lucy's place?" Arthur asked.

"Alright."

"What did you do there?"

"Oh, you know, just hung out with Lucy and her friends, some of which happened to be people residing in my parent's neighbourhood," replied Michelle. "She is really doing it," Michelle continued.

"Doing what?" asked Arthur.

"You know, starting her own floral business. Michael is supporting her with this too," said Michelle.

"You never mentioned that Lucy is opening up her own business," said Arthur.

"Sure I have, we also talked about it at the wedding. Don't you remember?" asked Michelle.

"Nope."

Michelle sat there, feeling somewhat annoyed that Arthur often does not listen. It makes her feel as if what she has to say does not matter. Maybe she is not being interesting enough for Arthur.

Despite feeling that she may be to blame for Arthur not listening, she feels hurt by this action. "A-Arthur.." Michelle stutters attempting to express her feelings.

"Oh look," Arthur throws a smile in Michelle's direction, "The food is here."

Michelle was going to speak up about Arthur not listening. Again, not wanting to ruin the moment, she decides against it. Instead she sits there quietly as Arthur describes how he would like Michelle to design the house.

"Your father is a champion," Arthur presses on.

"How do you mean?"

"First of all, he does what he wants. He is such a cool cucumber. Your mother is great for going along with this. Giving him the freedom to do what he wants, despite his antics," Arthur trailed.

"What antics?"

Arthur stares at Michelle briefly then nods his head. "Nothing, they just seem like a great pair. Your father doing his thing, and your mother just going along with it. They are both so responsive, so likeable, and am excited to have them as in-laws," Arthur said.

Funny, Michelle does not see her parents like this at all. Maybe Arthur will feel differently once he has more exposure to them. Although it is a pleasure to see Arthur so happy now.

They continue to eat in silence, all of a sudden, Arthur shifts his focus to the casino area. "Hey Michelle, would you mind if we stayed here for awhile and check out the casino? You know how much I have a penchant for card games. There are also some rides in town. How about we check that out too? Maybe do a couple of the rides, and check out the panoramic city views?"

Michelle sighed subtly to herself. She was tired, not interested in attending the casino, nor doing the rides, and just wanted to return to the hotel room. In addition, Michelle did not know that Arthur enjoyed card games. This was news to her. She looked up to see Arthur waiting in anticipation for her response.

"Okay, I will join you at the casino. I don't think that I will last much longer tonight because, honestly, I am exhausted and would prefer to call it a night, and resume our activities tomorrow," Michelle replied.

"Sure, c'mon," Arthur said enthusiastically.

After they finished eating, Arthur and Michelle proceeded to the casino area. It smelled of leathers and stale beer. This odour was not appealing to Michelle, nor were the collection of drunk men strewn around that were staring at them both curiously. There was also a scattering of people that looked like tourists, and some that were dressed up, like they had just attended the theatre.

Arthur dashed over to the bar, and purchased two beers. At the bar, he began to converse with a group of people. It is as if Arthur had forgotten that he was here with Michelle. Why does Arthur always have such a short attention span? It is like one moment he is totally present with her, and the next, she may as well not exist. In her silent fuming, Michelle made her way to the bar and cleared her throat then stating, "Excuse me."

Arthur swung around, "Oh hey baby, I got caught up chatting with these folks from Texas. Here, I bought you a beer," Arthur handed Michelle the beer.

"Thanks," Michelle replied, whilst rolling her eyes.

As a group, they proceeded to one of the tables where a deck of cards were being distributed. Michelle stood in the background and watched as Arthur chatted away whilst playing with his group of new friends. Oh boy, they are in this casino for less than an hour, and already, Arthur has found a way to distract his attention from Michelle, lighting up the place with his charismatic nature. This is probably why they are drawn to each other. Their characters compliment each other: he – exuberant, social, capturing people's attention. Her, more reserved, reflective, being more in the background. Although, as she thinks this, she feels that this observation is not true, and that somehow she is compromising something – that is – not being true to herself, although she cannot put her finger on what this means exactly.

After a couple of rounds of cards, Michelle decides that she is ready to leave – for real this time. She taps Arthur on the shoulder, "Arthur, honey, I think I am going to head back to the hotel now."

"Already? We just got here."

"Well, not really. Between the restaurant and the casino, we have been here for about three hours."

"Well time flies when you're having fun," Arthur said.

Michelle disagrees, although she will not say this to Arthur. Instead she smiles, "yes, well I am ready to go Arthur, I am exhausted."

"Okay, honey, I'm not quite ready to go yet, we are right in the middle of this game, and still want to continue for a few more rounds. Plus I am on a roll! Isn't that true boys?" Arthur says to his company, teasingly.

"You bet!" responds one of the men.

Arthur turns and looks again at Michelle thoughtfully, "Here, I'll give you some cash, take a taxi back. I'll join you soon enough."

"Okay," said Michelle as she took the money Arthur handed to her. She looked up at Arthur, and they kissed. She started to walk toward the exit, feeling like she needed to compose herself before turning back and flashing Arthur a smile. He responds by tilting his head back slightly and waving at her. She left, and that feeling of loneliness returned to her.

The next day, the light rays from the sun poked at her eyelids, compelling Michelle to open her eyes. She found Arthur opening up the curtains. Michelle pulled herself up, leaning herself up against the headboard.

"Good morning," said Arthur with a raspy voice.

"You were smoking cigars last night, weren't you?" Michelle asked, smelling stale smoke from the night before.

"Oh, well, you know how it is. I get caught up having a good time, and out comes the spirits and the cigars," Arthur replied.

Michelle got out of bed, picking up her housecoat and wrapping it around her body. She gazed out of the window, finding beautiful ocean views and a beaming sun. "What would you like to do today?" Michelle asked.

"Well, there is a show in town, with acrobatics and other entertainers. I thought that might be fun to check out," Arthur responded.

"I was hoping that we could check out some of the shops. I wouldn't mind doing some shopping," Michelle intervened.

"Oh, well, we could do that too," Arthur agreed.

They took showers, got dressed, and ready for the day. In town, they decided to walk along a major shopping strip. Arthur seemed quite distracted most of the time.

"Is there anything wrong?" asked Michelle.

"No, nothing, just tagging along shopping with my old lady," Arthur smiled wryly.

Arthur decided that he wanted to check out a couple of cigar shops that he spotted across the street. Michelle was more interested in the clothing and jewelry shops. She was also thinking of shopping in the souvenir shops to pick up some things for her family.

"How about you come into these shops with me, and then I'll join you in the cigar shops?" Michelle suggested. Arthur agreed, although he seemed quite bored with the shopping experience. She would ask his opinion about things, and he would provide vague answers. Finally, Arthur excused himself, and they agreed that after he purchased his cigars, that he would go into the information centre and pick up a pamphlet regarding the show Arthur wanted to see later that day.

After they parted, Michelle decided that she was not being adventurous enough for Arthur. She noticed a lingerie shop, and went in with the intention of purchasing something sexy. After all, keeping her man's attention is her code from now on.

She went into the lingerie shop, browsing through all of the merchandise, looking carefully at each piece. She had an opaque shopping bag filled with things that she had purchased for herself and for her family. She decided to place the lingerie in this opaque bag so that Arthur would not see them. After making her purchases, she rummaged through her bag, strategically placing the items at the bottom so that Arthur would not see them. She went to join Arthur, and noticed him speaking with a very tall, attractive blonde across the street. The woman noticed Michelle staring at them curiously. Arthur followed the woman's glance, to find Michelle approaching him.

"Hi honey, this is Gloria. I just found out that she will be in the show tonight. She was just describing the various acts to me in detail."

"How about that," Michelle replied. "I'm Michelle, Arthur's wife."

"Oh, hello," Gloria responded, looking down at her shuffling feet. There was an awkward silence.

"Well, we should be going, right Arthur?" Michelle intervened.

"Yes, of course. See you in the show?" asked Arthur.

"Yes, I will be one of the performers tonight," Gloria replied.

"Great," Arthur replied.

Arthur and Michelle parted ways again, as he decided that he wanted to continue to browse the information shop for more details about the region. Michelle decided that she would go back to the room, and thought this to be a great opportunity to pick up some wine and get changed into the sexy lingerie she had just purchased. She was sure that this seduction would capture his attention enough to carry them both through into the night. She was so excited.

At the hotel, Michelle waited patiently for Arthur's arrival. Finally she heard the card swipe and he entered the room. Michelle was sitting at a table by the balcony window. It was a beautiful night with a full moon. She was wearing a long, flowing, deep red dress. She had spent much time doing her hair and makeup and had arranged for the hotel staff to bring up some chocolate covered strawberries and truffles. She had let the wine breathe for awhile on the table.

"Wow, you look stunning," gasped Arthur in awe.

"Thank you, I couldn't wait for you to return," Michelle replied.

"Are you ready for the show?" asked Arthur.

"Um, not quite…" Michelle proceeded to slip her dress off to reveal the lingerie she had purchased earlier.

Arthur looked at her, stunned silent for a moment, "W-wow," Arthur stammered then continued, "I must say that I was not expecting this. What has gotten into you? All of a sudden you are quite the seductress," Arthur observed.

"Well, I don't think I need an excuse to want to be with my husband," Michelle replied.

Arthur walked across the room, grabbing her. They kissed passionately, and made heated, passionate, frantic love on the hotel bed. Their bodies reflecting the intense moonlight pouring into the windows.

"You are trying to wear me out woman," Arthur stated, looking across the room at the clock. "I almost feel too tired to go to the show tonight," Arthur continued.

"Well, we can always stay in and have a quiet night, munching on the goodies that the staff brought up," Michelle contemplated.

Arthur walked toward the table and sat in one of the chairs.

"Wine?" asked Arthur.

"Sure," replied Michelle.

They both sat by the window for awhile sipping on wine and munching on the strawberries and truffles.

"You know, I am going to make you so happy Arthur," Michelle assured. "We finally will have an opportunity for a life together, you and me, in complete bliss," Michelle continued.

"Well, hopefully it will not be just you and I for long. I am excited to have two lovely and little ones running around," Arthur stated.

They spoke for awhile about their future, Arthur talking about his career and the hopes he had for a promotion, and more money to provide for them and their future children. Michelle spoke of her passion for keeping her husband happy with warm greetings at all times when he was not busy at work. They chatted and laughed by the balcony door and windows, enveloped in moonlight, Michelle felt validated, and felt a sense of fulfillment and freedom. So much so that she felt comfortable telling Arthur a secret about herself.

"Arthur, as your wife, I feel that it is important to tell you something."

"What is it?" Arthur asked.

"I have secretly been admiring Lucy's desire to maintain her independence with her partner. With her deciding to open her own floral business and all. The truth is, I would love to do something like that. It is not something I have told anyone, out of fear of being put down and discouraged," Michelle stated frankly.

"What kind of business?" Arthur asked.

"Handcrafts. It is something I have always loved to do. I guess Lucy has inspired me through her own description of her future plans," Michelle stated.

"Well, I don't know. You'll be awefully busy being a housewife, and even busier when you become a stay at home mother. After all, I am the one that plans on taking care of all the finances so that you won't have to work. Instead, you will have time to be there for me and our children," Arthur said.

"Well, what if I get bored doing that?" Michelle asked.

"What? Bored? With me?" Arthur probed.

"No, that is not what I mean. I just mean…"

"Look, Michelle, can we not discuss this some other time? We were supposed to be having a good time tonight. Don't you think you are jumping the gun springing this on me?" Arthur asks, raising is voice.

"I didn't mean to spring anything on you.." Michelle started to say.

"Listen, we better get going now if we want to see this show," Arthur interrupted. "Common, get dressed, we have to go," Arthur demanded. He got up abruptly to freshen up in the washroom. Michelle sat there feeling perplexed. A knot formed in her stomach. She followed Arthur in to the washroom once he was finished and freshened up herself. They both got dressed quietly, not saying much to each other on the way to the show.

At the show, there were a lot of people roaming about. The show was about to start and people were rushing to their seats. Her and Arthur had got there just in time. Music boomed and the hall vibrated from all of the reverberations. Then out came the entertainers wearing bright colours, scarves streaming from their bodies, sparkles twinkling from them, picking up the surrounding light and reflecting the same light into the room. The show was quite energetic, with lots of acrobats, singing, and instruments playing. During the intermission, Arthur excused himself leaving Michelle sitting there alone. After awhile, Michelle decided that she would take note of where they are seated and head to the ladies washroom. On her way, she caught Arthur speaking with Gloria, the woman they had seen and that Arthur was talking to earlier on the street. They were in close proximity to each other, their faces only a few inches apart.

"Arthur," Michelle said as she approached them.

"Oh, hi honey. You remember Gloria don't you? She is one of the entertainers this evening. Didn't she look fabulous up there, and talented to boot!" Arthur commented.

"Yes, I remember. Listen, I was just going to use the ladies room. You remember where we are seated don't you? I took note of where our seats are in case you had forgotten," stated Michelle.

"Yes, I remember. I'll see you soon. Gloria was just telling me an interesting story about her experiences on the road with the group," Arthur said. Gloria looked over at Michelle, smiling slyly.

"Yes, of course. I'll see you…later" Michelle said. She wasn't finished her sentence and Arthur was already back conversing with Gloria. She walked away, feeling as though Arthur had barely noticed her exit.

The second act had begun, and Michelle found her seat.

Arthur was not there. About halfway through the second act, Arthur appeared, climbing over people's legs to return to his seat. He sat down, and Michelle could smell a whif of ladies perfume. She sat there feeling uneasy, and in silence.

The rest of the honeymoon was fairly uneventful. Michelle found that she was spending more and more time on her own, scoping out the town, or lounging on the beach. The night before their departure, the two of them had made arrangements to have dinner. Michelle was excited that they would have some quality time to spend together before returning home. Michelle had to find her own way to the restaurant; Arthur had insisted that she go by taxi and that Arthur would cover the expense when she arrived.

At the restaurant, Arthur was at the bar, chatting with a new group of people. He barely noticed Michelle as she approached. Then, he finally noticed her.

"Oh, hi sweetie. These boys are from Texas. We seem to be meeting a lot of Texans, don't we? I was just telling them about my experiences in Texas when I've gone there for business. Just saying what a beautiful state it is," Arthur said.

"Yes, your hubby here seems to know quite a bit about our great state," said one man.

"We were just describing authentic Texan cuisine," said another man.

"Say, do you like to cook?" asked another man to Michelle.

"Oh, I love being in the kitchen. I'll admit that I don't know much about preparing Texan cuisine though," Michelle said. "Arthur, honey, I think our table is ready," Michelle informed Arthur under her breath.

"Of course. Boys, great chatting with you," Arthur said giving them a half wave as he and Michelle walked away from them and toward their table.

After being seated, Arthur said that he had already ordered for the two of them. Michelle was delighted at Arthur's manliness, taking charge. She felt like a woman again. Once the food came, they both dove in. Michelle realized that she had not eaten all day and was starving.

"Don't indulge too much," Arthur warned, "The last thing I need is a fat wife," Arthur continued.

Michelle smiled, and they sat quietly, seemingly not having much to say to each other during their meal. After awhile, Michelle cleared her throat and asked, "What really interests you Arthur?"

"What do you mean?" Arthur replied.

"Oh, you know, generally, what are you passionate about?"

"What am I passionate about?" Arthur echoed, "Everything that I do," he answered.

"Well, I would say that I am passionate about one-to-one interactions. I really like to get to the heart of what people are interested in," Michelle reflected.

"I like robust crowds, really engaging with a group. You'll have to saddle up, as you will be accompanying me to many business events. Not to mention all of the house parties we will be hosting. You had better build on your cooking skills darling," Arthur commanded.

"Well, I hope that is balanced out with some one-to-one time. I much rather have quiet time, be it over a nice cup of tea, sharing stories, or watching a great movie. Some time out in nature is good too. Time to reflect, and take it all in," Michelle said dreamily.

"Reflect? Sounds boring to me. You have not got out of your shell enough. That will change, under my influence. Although we do compliment each other, you being more quiet and reserved, me more social and exuberant," Arthur said.

"Well, I can be exuberant too you know. Let's…" Michelle started to elaborate before being interrupted by Arthur.

"I've noticed our new friends are still at the bar. Should we offer to share our table with them?" Arthur asked.

"I don't know Arthur, I was hoping that.."

"Hey, boys!" Arthur yelled across the room, capturing their attention, "Why don't you come and join us!"

The men approached their table, and Arthur busied himself pushing another table against their table, and helping the men to gather chairs. They all resumed their prior conversation about Texas, and Arthur was excited to learn that his next business trip there is in one of the men's hometown. They chattered adamantly for what seemed like forever to Michelle. She joined in briefly, and meekly when she could get a word in.

"Well, at least you can be assured that your old lady is not going to cheat on you. She doesn't seem like the type. Kudos to you for knowing how to pick 'em brother," said one of the men.

Michelle sat there, feeling like something had suppressed her vocal cords. Unable to speak up, she sat there feeling bewildered. As they got up to leave, Michelle felt like she had the weight of the world on her shoulders. Her honeymoon was not what she had hoped it would be. She also felt that in the limited time that she had with Arthur, they did not actually have as much in common as she would have hoped. Maybe Arthur is right, maybe she is too boring. She made a vow to herself the next day as they got on the plane that she would do all that she could to please Arthur, by making him happy through the efforts that she will make to conform to who he would like her to be. She is his wife now, that is her identity, and it is now her mission to conform to what he believes in and values, and to fit his picture of reality. In her mind, this is the only way that she will keep his interest and ensure that she is dazzling enough to hold his heart.

Chapter 11: The Affair

Upon their return Arthur went back to work immediately. As it turned out, Arthur had formed a partnership with Michelle's father that enhanced his career opportunities. Michelle went to work fixing up their new house, making it nice, and creating a home for them both. Jennifer would visit Michelle often after school, and Jennifer continued to have difficulties with Christopher. On one such visit, Jennifer was particularly distraught as it looked as if Christopher had put the make on Nancy – Jennifer's so-called best friend; this time for good.

Michelle had prepared an early dinner for them as she was unsure what time Arthur would be home that night. He was travelling a lot and Michelle was grateful for the company as she felt that the house was big, quiet, and lonely a lot of the time. As they were sitting in the dining area eating, Jennifer was lamenting about her failed relationship.

"I don't know what to do now. It seems as if they are together for keeps. Can you believe her? Talk about backstabbing!" Jennifer whined.

"Well, to be honest with you, I am surprised that you remained friends with her after her prior shananigans with Christopher. That should have been your big red flag," Michelle commented.

"I know, but I was hoping that things would change since she realized that I was hip to her having eyes for my boyfriend. I can't *believe* her, I mean, he was my guy," Jennifer replied.

"I think possession will get you into trouble from the start," Michelle said.

"My guy," Jennifer repeated. "What do you mean possession will get me into trouble? How so?" Jennifer inquired.

"Oh, I don't know. I think that when you hold onto something it is more likely to become lost on you. Men can detect desperation from a mile away. Besides, you deserve so much better than that. Do you really want to be with someone who cheats on you? It means that you cannot trust him. Things are doomed from that point right there," Michelle said.

"I really am happy to be with the in-crowd, regardless of how I am treated. Although, this hurts so much that I feel kind of lost...,"

Jennifer said and then trailed off. She started looking at a picture of Arthur and Michelle that was mounted on the wall in the dining area. "You two are so lucky. I wish I could keep a man's attention the way you keep Arthur's. He also has some great advice, very wise. I should have listened to him before," Jennifer said.

"Well, you know what they say, hindsight is twenty-twenty," Michelle replied.

As they finished eating, Michelle could hear Arthur's keys in the door.

"Oh my, speak of the devil. What a pleasant surprise to have him come home so early," Michelle stated. She got up to greet Arthur as he walked into the house.

"Hi honey!" Arthur said cheerfully.

"Hi yourself," Michelle replied.

They hugged tightly.

"My sister is here. We decided to have an early dinner this evening as I was unsure when you would be returning home," Michelle explained.

Jennifer emerged from the dining room and went to hug Arthur. "Hi handsome, we were just talking about you," Jennifer said with a smile.

"Well, nothing outrageous I hope," Arthur replied with a wink.

Michelle decided that she would do the washing up. Jennifer offered to help; Michelle declined this offer as she assumed that her and Arthur probably had some catching up to do. After all, neither one of them had seen much of Arthur since returning from their honeymoon.

"You two go ahead and chat. I am sure that you have some catching up to do. I'll put on a pot of tea," Michelle said.

"Okay, sure," Arthur replied. He looked over at Jennifer, "I should show you some of the knick knacks we bought while away," Arthur said.

"Oh, well Michelle has already shown me quite a bit," Jennifer replied.

"Yes, well I am sure that you have not seen everything. Come, you have a seat in the living area and I will be back in a flash," Arthur instructed.

"Sure," Jennifer agreed.

Michelle worked diligently bringing dishes from the dining area into the kitchen, and then proceeded to wash them. She could hear mumbled voices from the living area; she was curious to know what they were talking about yet could not make out what they were saying. She pulled out a tray to mount the teapot and cups on and headed toward the living area. As she was standing in the entrance way, she stopped in her tracks and observed her sister and her husband, talking adamantly, their shoulders rubbing. There was a fan of merchandise spread on the floor, mostly Arthur's purchases from the cigar shop, and general collector's items.

"The tea is ready. Help yourself, I will bring in the pound cake from the kitchen," Michelle interrupted.

"So, you really are a brave one, making the decision to leave Christopher for good this time. That really takes guts," Arthur commented as Michelle re-entered the room.

"Yes, well we were just talking about that Arthur," Michelle informed. "I was saying that it is about time because Christopher has never treated her right," Michelle said.

"Yes, well we know that politeness runs in the family. At least she had the assertiveness to vocalize her concerns," Arthur said staring at Jennifer then continued, "I am so proud of you!"

Jennifer stared back, blushing. "Yes, well your great advice provided me with strength. What would I do without you?" Jennifer said with a tone of desperation.

"Well, we both know that you'll be just fine," Michelle replied.

"You sure will. Such a strong and assertive woman. I love that about you. You are a real go-getter. Even though things did not work out between you and Christopher, you are still standing strong," Arthur said.

"Not to change the subject, but I heard that you finally had the chance to see that show in the Carolinas that you have been raving about. Michelle mentioned that to me," Jennifer said to Arthur.

"Yes, it was great! Your sister was awfully quiet during the show though. I was somewhat surprised given all the festivities. It was such an exciting atmosphere to be in," Arthur said.

"Well, Michelle is just that way. More reserved. Isn't that right sis?" Jennifer asked looking at Michelle mischieviously.

"You are right Jennifer, I prefer doing things that are more quiet, and not quite so chaotic, although I was grateful to just be there with my husband. Especially compared to now, with Arthur being so busy with work and all," Michelle replied.

"I hear ya, sis. Man, if I was there, I would totally be taking it all in, and interacting with every person, place, and thing that I can get my hands on! It is not everyday that one has the opportunity to attend a show like that, and with such a hottie to boot," Michelle said, then winked at Arthur.

"I know. You and I definitely have extroversion in common. I would go nutty spending too much time alone, or having too much quiet time - period," Arthur agreed.

"Yes, well, I have my own ideas of what fun looks like," Michelle murmured.

"Speaking of taking it all in, there is a street festival in the city centre tonight. How about we head over there soon?" asked Arthur.

"Oh, I don't know honey. I'm pretty tired. I think I'll just finish my tea, and maybe read a book before retiring to bed," Michelle replied.

"Well, I'm up for it. Sounds like fun!" Jennifer replied.

"Great! We should head out soon so we don't miss out on too much," Arthur suggested.

"Okay!" Jennifer said as she sprung up and then went to retrieve her things. Arthur followed her.

Michelle sat there, surprised that they were both going to just leave her there. Oh well, what will be, will be. Arthur walked toward Michelle and kissed her on the cheek.

"We shouldn't be out too late," Arthur said.

"Oh sure. See you later," Michelle replied.

As it turned out, they both stayed out quite late. Michelle had just gone to bed after sitting by the window, reading, waiting for Arthur to return. She was upset that he had stayed out so late, and was unsure who with. She assumed that Arthur dropped Jennifer off hours ago, since she had school in the morning. As Arthur entered the room, Michelle pretended that she was asleep. Arthur wanted her in bed that night, and Michelle shrugged him off, turning the front of her body opposite to Arthur's body. Soon enough, they were both asleep.

Michelle felt more and more alienated as time went on. Jennifer was coming around the house less and less, and Arthur continued to work long hours. Arthur had invited Michelle to numerous work functions; Michelle always had an excuse for not attending. The truth was that she was not up for attending all of these social events. First off, she resented that her father was monopolizing Arthur's time with work. Second, Michelle was afraid of feeling left out at these events. Thinking back about their honeymoon, Arthur was out and about flurrying around effortlessly with his wondrous social skills. While he was exerting his talents in this area, Michelle felt awkward and stifled. She never really knew what to say; at least it seemed that way. She often felt that she had to make an effort to carry on a conversation, and just felt that compared to Arthur – and even to her sister, she did not measure up. She had also discovered – even more so since they were married, how much of a ladies man Arthur is. He is always charming the ladies, and Michelle resents that women hang off of him, flirting madly. Do they not have any shame, doing this right in front of his wife?

On one such occasion, her and Arthur were hosting a dinner in their home. Michelle had toiled for hours preparing the main dishes, finger foods, and desserts. Lucy and Michael had been invited, and for once, Michelle was glad that Lucy would be close by as this famiiarity provided a source of comfort for Michelle. When the day of the dinner came, Michelle felt somewhat under the weather. How was she supposed to be the star hostess now feeling the way that she does?

Thankfully, Lucy and Michael arrived early and their company hclpcd mitigate the anxiety for Lucy, albeit only for a short while. Michelle was contemplating getting everything set up and then making her excuses to go upstairs and rest for the night.

"You do look kind of peaky Michelle," Lucy observed. "How is married life treating you?"

"Oh, it is fine. I'm at home mostly, and Arthur is so busy with work. I feel like time is just racing by," Michelle replied.

"Well, we see Arthur all over the place. Michael and I go out quite a bit together. In fact, we have seen him with Jennifer a lot these days," Lucy commented.

"Out with Jennifer? During the day?" Michelle asked.

"Yes, we've seen him picking her up from school, and dropping her home. Sometimes he will drop her off at home later too, like they had been out for awhile." Lucy looked over at Michelle, "I thought that you knew that they were spending a lot of time together?" Lucy inquired.

"Yes, of course I know. I mean, generally speaking. I don't believe in policing Arthur's time. I trust him," Michelle stated.

"Oh sure. Well if you need us to help you out at all tonight, let us know," Lucy offered.

"Will do," Michelle replied.

The truth was that Michelle was not aware that Arthur was spending any time with Jennifer apart from when she came to visit in their home. Neither one of them had mentioned this, and their outings could explain why Jennifer had been coming around the house less often. All of a sudden, Michelle felt very uncomfortable because Jennifer is one of their guests this evening. This fact coupled with already feeling anxious about having twenty or so people over (mostly Arthur's friends and colleagues) for dinner made her feel awashed with a sense of inadequacy. As the guests started to arrive, Arthur followed them in with Jennifer following closely behind Arthur. She was giggling and chattering on like a school-girl, carelessly handing Michelle a bunch of flowers.

"For you sis!" Jennifer exclaimed.

"Thanks," Michelle mumbled awkwardly.

"Are mom and dad coming tonight? I mean, I know that Arthur and dad share colleagues, and part of me assumed that they would be attending.

"Yes, I think that they might be," Jennifer replied.

"Who drove you here?" Michelle asked.

"Arthur."

"Oh."

"Cheer up sis, this is a party! You should be delighted!" Jennifer stated.

"Well, I'm not feeling very well, I'm afraid. I think that I may just head upstairs shortly.."

"You're kidding! That's too bad," Jennifer stated.

"Lucy!" Michelle called out.

Lucy came toward Michelle immediately, "How are you feeling?"

"Not that great. I think I will take you up on your offer to help out if that is okay with you. Sorry to do this, I know you are both guests," Michelle said.

"Oh, not at all Michelle. Besides, Michael has a talent for hosting. Just show us where everything is and we will go from there," Lucy replied.

"This way," Michelle replied. Michelle showed Michael and Lucy around mechanically, occasionally glancing over at her sister. She could really light up a room with her charisma. People were flocking around her like there is no tomorrow. She secretly envied this, and at the same time felt relieved to slip away into the quiet sanctuary that is her room. She walked lightly up the stairs and closed the door. She dozed off to sleep hearing the buzz of fun echoing from downstairs. Her parents had attended after all; both had come up briefly to check on her.

"You had better be careful," her father warned. "You may not be able to keep your husband's attention with the short attention span he has. Use your mother as an example, she always stands by me no matter what and makes her presence known. That is probably the main reason why we are still together," her father said.

"I know daddy, I know," Michelle replied. She looked over at her mother who smiled sympathetically.

"Well, you get some rest dear. We will be right downstairs if you need us," her mother assured.

"Thank you," replied Michelle who proceeded to doze off. They exited the room, closing the door behind them. Michelle shook at the impact of the door closing, the smell of their presence heightened and entrenched in her nostrils.

After the event, the house resumed its quiet air. Michelle had been feeling persistently worse and worse; she was not forthcoming about this to Arthur, who did not seem to notice since he was not around much. There was the occasional interaction when he managed to come home early enough for dinner and when Michelle could stay up late. They also had regular, yet brief interactions in the morning before Arthur left for work. One morning, Michelle decided that she would ask Arthur about picking up Jennifer from school on a regular basis.

"Arthur, I have to ask you something," Michelle stated.

Arthur looked up from his paper, glancing over at Michelle. "Sure, you know that you can ask me anything," Arthur replied.

"Lucy mentioned that you have been picking Jennifer up from school a lot. She also mentioned that she has seen you two around town. Is this true?" Michelle asked.

"Oh, you know, I am just trying to be a good brother-in-law. Just trying to be supportive given all that she has been through recently," Arthur replied.

"Is there anything else that I should know?" Michelle asked.

"Like what?" Arthur asked.

"Like, how come you are spending so much time with her? This doesn't make sense to me. How do you find the time with your work schedule, not to mention all the travelling that you do?" Michelle prompted.

"Well, of course it makes sense. I have the car, so it is easy for me to pick her up. Besides, she trusts me enough to confide in me. I thought that you would think that to be a good thing," Arthur replied.

"Yes, I suppose you are right," Michelle replied.

"See, I knew you would see things my way," Arthur said with a smile. He looked at his watch, "I have to go," he said with one raised eyebrow, "Duty calls." He reached in kissing Michelle quickly and began to gather his things before leaving.

"I have not been feeling that great, and wanted to let you know that I'll be seeing my doctor today for a check up," Michelle informed Arthur.

"Do you still have that bug? Do you want me to drive you?"

"No, that is okay, the appointment is not until later. Could I get some money for a cab?" Michelle asked.

"Yes, of course." Arthur provided her with some money and then exited the house.

Michelle piddled around the house for awhile after Arthur left. Before leaving, the phone rang.

"Hello?"

"Yes, hello Michelle, it is Lucy."

"Oh, hi Lucy, how are you?"

"I'm okay, thank you. Are you feeling better?"

"Not really, I am heading to the doctor today actually. I am long overdue for a check up," Michelle replied.

"Okay, well, I think that we need to talk about something. Are you able to come over after your appointment?"

"Sure, the doctor's office is not too far from where you live. I will walk over afterwards," Michelle replied.

Upon Michelle's visit with the doctor, she learned that she was pregnant. Oh how excited, and scared Michelle was to learn this. Arthur will be delighted, as he has been wanting to have children for the longest time. At least as long as she has known him.

"Be sure to go to the pharmacy next door to obtain your pre-natal vitamins. Also, here is a list of foods to avoid while pregnant. You will make a fantastic mother. Congratulate Arthur for me as well," the doctor said.

"Yes, I will. Thank you."

Michelle went over to see Lucy immediately after seeing the doctor and running her errands. Lucy ushered her into the house quickly.

"Where's Michael?"

"At work. Listen, I have to talk to you about something," Lucy urged.

"What is it Lucy?"

"It's about Arthur and Jennifer."

"What about them?"

"He is cheating on you. With Jennifer."

"What?"

"We have continued to spot them around town. The other day, we saw them kissing on the street."

"Are you sure it was them?"

"Yes, of course I am sure. They were looking pretty cozy together, as if this has been going on for awhile. To be honest, I suspected that something was going on between them. It seemed strange that they were spending so much time together," Lucy remarked.

Michelle sank into the chair, not wanting to believe Lucy and yet knowing it to be true. She had suspected this may be happening and instead of acknowledging this suspicion, she denied it, stuffing the feelings deep inside. She looked up at Lucy, "You cannot say a word to Arthur about this."

"What? Why?" Lucy said with a puzzled expression.

"First of all, this is my business. Second of all, I am pregnant."

"You are? How far along?"

"Yes I am. I just found out today, and I am a couple of months along. I'll handle this the way I see fit," Michelle remarked.

"Bastard. How could he do this to you, and at this crucial time too, when you are both about to become parents," Lucy said with disgust.

"I know. Promise me that you will say nothing of this? Let me handle it," Michelle said desperately.

"Okay. If you need anything, you let me know," Lucy said.

"I will."

Michelle went home that afternoon, vowing to herself that she would not let either one of them know about their affair. Once her pregnancy was announced, Michelle got temporary relief as now the attention was on her. Everyone tending to her every need: her parents were ecstatic to welcome their first grandchild into the world, and Arthur was beside himself with the excitement of becoming a father. For awhile Arthur was taking time off work to be home with Michelle. Michelle was adamant about not having Jennifer over at the house, and managed to conjure up various excuses for why this should be so.

The excitement wore off for Arthur rather quickly as Michelle progressed in her pregnancy and he began to resume spending a lot of time at work. One day, Michelle was feeling adventurous and decided to surprise Arthur at work. She entered his office and was surprised that his assistant was not there. The waiting area was very quiet and Arthur's door was cracked open. She heard whispers and what sounded like shuffling noises. Michelle's stomach was doing flip flops as she approached his door, and it felt as if her heart was pulsating intensively in her throat area. When she peaked inside, she found her husband and Jennifer completely naked, going at it wildly on top of his office desk. He grabbed at her passionately and they began thrusting at each other against the wall. Michelle was devastated, and was all seized up. She backed away slowly and did not realize until she felt a dampness on her hands that tears were streaming down her face. She found a ladies washroom and walked into one of the washroom stalls, sinking to the floor. She sobbed there quietly for awhile before proceeding to the sink to splash some water on her face. On her way out of the building, Michelle discovered a coffee shop and decided to stop in and buy a tea. She sat with her tea, and stared out the window. Not wanting to go home, and not knowing what to do, Michelle lingered in the coffee shop and decided to purchase another tea. As she turned around to sit down again, she spotted Jennifer leaving the building. This was her chance to confront her husband now that Jennifer was gone. How could he do this to her? Has she not been the best wife she can be? Does he really hate her that much that he could be so contemptable? As for Jennifer, what kind of a sister is she, and who does she think she is? Out of all the men that are available and at her fingertips, why her husband? She felt demoralized and betrayed. How could she face her sister again? Was she going to continue to lie to her face as she has been? Do mom and dad know? Is this why her father made the comment about keeping Arthur's attention, because he knew that Arthur was sleeping with Jennifer?

All of these thoughts swirled around in Michelle's head. She decided to purchase another tea for Arthur, and head back to his office. As she approached his office, Michelle spotted him zipping up his trousers and re-buckling his belt. He saw Michelle approaching, and appeared jumpy.

"Michelle, what are you doing here?"

"Nice to see you too. I thought I would surprise you. Look, I brought you a tea."

"Oh thanks honey. Listen, I really have a lot of work to catch up on," Arthur said.

"I know, you are usually very busy. I noticed you changing, what's the occasion?" Michelle asked.

"Oh nothing, your father and I had a round of squash earlier, and I figured I would freshen up. 'Tis the advantage of having my own office," Arthur replied.

"I know," Michelle replied. There was an awkward silence. "What are you working on these days?" Michelle asked.

"Since when are you interested in the work I do?"

"Since now."

"Well, we can talk more about it later. I have some reports I need to submit today. How about I make it a priority to come home early tonight and we can have dinner together? Or better yet, I'll take you out."

"No, I do not want to go out. I'd like a quiet evening at home alone with my husband," Michelle replied.

"Yes, of course. I'll see you later," Arthur said.

Michelle stared at him for a few moments.

"Why are you looking at me like that?"

"Are you happy? I mean, with me?"

"Of course I am. I married you didn't I? It is just that someone has to put food on the table, and I need my fun too, since you're not too big on painting the town red."

Fun? What did he mean by fun? Is he alluding to this repulsive affair that he is having with her sister? She did not have the nerve to ask, and instead, made her excuses and headed home.

Michelle carried on as if the affair was not happening. She was not yet ready to confront anyone, including her own conflicts. For if she confronted herself, she was afraid of falling apart and no longer playing the role of good and loyal wife to Arthur: low maintenance and as reliable as the sun. She felt somewhat at fault, after all, she was not as flamboyant, exuberant, and sultry as Jennifer. On the other hand, she felt that fate had stepped in and that it was inevitable that Arthur would have wandering eyes. Maybe her father was right, maybe men are not meant to be with just one woman. Look at Jennifer, she was not able to capture Christopher's attention for long. She also thought about her upbringing – and that she was never given the opportunity to find her own voice. She was never given the opportunity to speak up for herself and articulate what she believed in. She relied so heavily on being the rock, holding everything together, and managing well that she has lost sight of who she truly is. She was so afraid of losing all and being locked up that she felt unequipped to do anything, other than to pretend that this affair was not happening, that she was satisfied, and that all is well. She felt trapped, lost in a sea of problems in her head, and in her circumstances with seeming inability to do anything about it. So she decided that she would throw her hands up and just accept that this is the way that her life is meant to be. That she was meant to be trapped, no matter what the situation is and that nothing will ever change. All she could do is be strong, plaster a smile of her face, and get on with things. She would continue to wear her mask of invincibility and that would carry her through.

Chapter 12: Discussion with her Soul Family

Back with her Soul family in her power pyramid of light, she dwells with a feeling of intense sadness. What a tragic sequence of events. The demoralization of all the events leaving an energetic blue print of despair.

She feels the love of her Soul family as she sits with this sea of emotions running through her energetic grid. She feels her soulmates sending her love light energy; the energy of healing that she needs to proceed with a dialogue of pure honesty.

"We know your thoughts and feelings, for we are One," states one of her guides.

"You need not despair any longer, we will always be here to love and support you," says another.

"You now have a choice to make. Do you wish to return to the Earth plane for another sojourn?" asks another.

"I don't know if I can go through another incarnation of intense pain. If that is the life that I will have to endure again, I am considering staying in the ether indefinitely. To return to the Earth seems like it would be cruel and unusual punishment. I don't know if I could survive that," the one known as Michelle in her prior life replies.

"Before you make a final decision, let us call in the beloved ones who took the sojourn with you in your prior life. They journeyed down with you as they too had issues that were out of balance that needed to be healed," states one of her guides.

The other Beings entered her pyramid of light with the power of thought and intention. For they had witnessed this screening from their respective dwellings in the cosmos.

"We know that it was a difficult lifetime for you. We understand the pain that you had to go through. We agreed to play out this karmic dance with you as we reflected your issues, just as you reflected ours, both positive and negative," stated the Earthly partner known as Arthur in their prior life.

"What are my issues? Please explain them to me so that I can have a deeper understanding," the one formerly known as Michelle asks as she turns to one of the Ascended Masters that she inadvertently called to in her nightly dreams on the Earth.

Her masters and guides regard each other, knowing that it is time to discuss what is apparent to them.

"This is in no particular order, we will reveal what we know to you and as directed by Source. First, you drew to you people in your life who try to control you by giving you their power and making you responsible for them. The most poignant example is the relationship you had with your younger sister, Jennifer." Michelle looks over at Jennifer in her pyramid and Michelle feels instant forgiveness and peace as she feels the loving intention between them.

"Jennifer was mirroring to you the need to be the rock in the family and to have a sense of control through taking responsibility for her. This occurred in multiple ways: in her relationship with Christopher, you felt that you had failed as a sister because she was not heeding your advice. You would do her schoolwork for her feeling that in order for her to succeed, you would have to take her actions, and do the leg work for her. Whenever you would second guess your self, and become in touch with your intuitive capacities that told you, this is not right, and not your responsibility – you would falter and give in to Jennifer's manipulative tactics. That is – guilting you into taking on her tasks as she knew that this strategy was effective in enabling her to shirk her responsibilities."

Another guide chimed in, "You also had people in your life who always tried to control you and take away your power. This was demonstrated in your relationship with Arthur. He always put his needs before yours. His issue was that he wanted immediate self-gratification. When you did not provide this to him, then he would withdraw his attention and affection. He knew that this would create a sense of insecurity in you, since your marriage to him was your only saving grace from your home environment. You wanted to get away from your immediate family and were willing to do anything to achieve that goal. What you did not consciously realize is that you were really wanting to get away from shouldering the responsibility of others. Responsibilities that were not your own. Instead of realizing that other people's actions are not your responsibility, you channeled your energy and focal point on creating a new life with Arthur. Through denying the truth behind the situation in your immediate family, and evading your own beliefs and values, you created the consequence of compromising your integrity rendering yourself powerless over your actions within the relationship with Arthur. This dynamic was mirrored to you more strongly when Arthur had an affair with your sister. He was providing the sense of security you were seeking by providing you with enough attention earlier in the relationship through the home you created, as well as through physical means. This was enough to keep you holding on to the delusion that things would change if you would stay silent about the wrong done to you rather than stand up to him and for yourself and create standards for the way in which you deserved to be treated. The thought of losing your home, and the relationship with Arthur was enough to keep you silenced. The longer you stayed in silence – which was for the rest of your life – the more lines were crossed and you missed the opportunity to take back your power."

"This brings us to the opportunity for freedom rather than comfort – the latter of which you chose to focus on," stated one of the ascended masters. "By turning a blind eye to the infidelity and the manipulative tactics surrounding you, you heightened your fear of stepping outside of your comfort zone because you feared failure. You created the illusion of being trapped due to not taking a stance and standing up for what you believed in. Beliefs for which you had denied and were actually not entirely aware of. Your inner power had become lost on you as you succumbed to the fear of the unknown and of failure. This also set the tone for robbing yourself of the opportunity to be a success in your relationships with Arthur, Jennifer, your parents, and in general. Remember that when you incarnate, your family agrees to play out the game of life with you in the third dimensional environment. This is the starting place for you to work out the issues you have, and sets the foundation for building on your strengths, and clearing away your limitations. Through holding on to fear, you then eliminated the chance to pursue the things in your life that you desired to engage in. For example, you have tremendous creative talents that you would occasionally ponder and maybe even create a business for yourself. You were so focused on satisfying the needs of others, that you forgot the talents within you and sacrificed this in an attempt to catch or hold on to validation via external means. This prevented you from successfully transcending that dynamic to come into your own and to become a success in the way that you are capable and desired to."

"Avoidance became a theme that grew stronger throughout your lifetime," stated another spirit guide. "Building on the theme of staying in your comfort zone out of fear of failure is using illness as a way to get out of a situation or feeling that the only way that you will get attention is by becoming ill. An example of the former that we witnessed on the screen is during group or social gatherings, particularly when Lucy was involved. You see, Lucy was actually mirroring positive attributes that reside within you such as independence, creativity, intelligence, and assertiveness derived from strong communication skills. You did not believe that you have these attributes, and instead compared yourself to her, wishing to be like her and feeling that that was unattainable. What you had forgotten is that her talents are also your talents. Lucy had a presence in your life to demonstrate this to you so that you would have the opportunity to get in touch with that part of yourself. Whenever Lucy attempted to get you involved in her circle, you would use illness as an excuse to avoid being in that circle, and as a way of avoiding the opportunity to tap into the potential that lies within.

An example of the latter is the way in which you interacted with Arthur. Whenever you felt that his attention was waning, such as during your honeymoon, and during your suspicions about his affair with Jennifer, you would go to illness as a method of capturing Arthur's attention. This would work in the short-term; however, notice that his attention on you never lasted and you would cycle between the gratification of obtaining his undivided attention and you chasing after it – often through illness.

Your tendency to use illness as an excuse to get out of a situation or to get attention was not done intentionally, but rather was done because you felt a great responsibility for those around you. You often felt pressured to measure up to other people's expectations and when this demand became unbearable then you would go to illness as an outlet. Kind of like taking a vacation from your life circumstances, namely from your immediate family, Arthur, and social circle."

"All of the issues we mention then brought you to blame others," stated another guide. "From dissatisfaction with yourself, and with your life in general, you began to blame those around you for how you felt rather than taking responsibility for your choices, behaviours, and actions. This was especially the case throughout the duration of your marriage because things were not going the way that you wanted them to. This brought you back to your childhood and feeling that if your parents gave you more freedom and did not always make you responsible for everything, that your life would be different. As an adult, fully capable of taking different actions, and making different choices, you focused on external circumstances such as your parents and blamed your upbringing on the dealings for which you chose to involve yourself in as an adult. This in turn, strengthened your perception of being powerless to change your situation and you stayed in problems which then blocked you from seeking out solutions."

"Where do I go from here? I don't see why I would willingly descend back to the Earth and the third dimensional environment and carry all this baggage with me, only to repeat the same painful experiences again," asked the one formerly known as Michelle.

"You have asked a very important question," states one of the ascended masters. "Think of spiritual growth like you would progressing through formal education. You cannot understand or experience more advanced concepts without going through less advanced, more fundamental stages. By going through the necessary training and experience, you build a foundation for yourself to stand on that then leads you to mastery. Liken it to embarking on becoming an expert professional on the Earth plane. Before you get there, you need to go through grade school, then college or university, and perhaps an apprenticeship. After this is complete, you then embark on gaining experience in your respective field and lifelong learning pursuits to further refine your skills. Spiritual growth and development parallels this concept."

"Oh, yes, now I am beginning to understand," the one formerly known as Michelle replies.

"The first step on your path to spiritual growth is journeying inward to obtain the answers that you would otherwise seek by external means. Being on the Earth plane is a powerful environment to enable this to happen because – although material gifts are a blessing, they are not all that is. Eventually there will be an internal push as you realize that there is more than just what is in front of you," the master continues. "The first step is that you begin searching out the origins of your emotional responses to pain. In your case, you had a strong sense of helplessness because you were not happy with the way your life was going. In turn, this conjured up deep-seated resentment especially toward your parents as you blamed them for your choices and behaviours rather than taking responsibility for your life, the need for satisfaction was not fulfilled in your marriage with Arthur because he was not behaving in the way you would have liked, and instead of standing up for yourself you clung onto the material benefits such as the house, regular income he was providing, and the attention he did provide you albeit not consistently. What was starving in you was the need for an authentic connection, and when that was not forthcoming, your felt scarcer and scarcer overtime and felt the only way you could survive is by hanging in there rather than taking a stand. This innate need to survive in a situation that brought you much unhappiness heightened your insecurity about yourself and your life. Throughout your life you continued to judge yourself by other people's standards and when they did not respond the way you wanted you unlovingly judged yourself. This led not only to blaming others for your actions but also to blaming yourself for other people's actions. All of these factors combined led to lack of vitality within you as you strived to manage well.

When you are provided with the gift of life on the Earth plane, surrounded by its respective physical and material presence and begin to realize that there is more than what is in front of you, you then become willing to look at the aspects of your ego self or things lurking under the subconscious and examine how your emotional beliefs control and direct you through your ego desires and needs. You see, the ego is an important part of who we are with respect to survival; however, it is not meant to be the director in all of our affairs. When you journey inward and seek out the wisdom beyond the physical you then begin the process of healing your emotional wounds. You then tap into new found strength, develop courage and use your inner power to speak your truth and stand in your integrity. Once these positive attributes start to become utilized, you gain momentum in stimulating yourself into action to manifest all you desire and to live your highest potential. With the help of your angels and guides who are always there to direct, support, and love you.

When you begin to take a stand and set the intention to

overcome fear, then you begin to realize that fear is not the enemy, but rather serves as a prompt that you can learn from, move through, and grow from. In this way, you will overcome the lower frequencies you experienced and that we have discussed, lower frequencies, which have controlled and shackled you in confinement of your own making. This also involves letting go of the need to control or dominate anyone else. For a need to control or dominate – whatever its form - stems from fear. Here are some of the gifts of journeying inward to realize your potential:

You will have the power to express freely, your beliefs and desires to those around you. You will not have dense thoughts and feelings weighing you down thus improving upon your health, vitality, and well-being. The words used are one of the most powerful tools on the Earth plane. Much like thoughts - when you speak, the words you choose send out energies that will help or hinder you. You will have the power to communicate words that uplift and aid in the creation of your desires without sabotaging your efforts. Through communicating and connecting with us regularly during your next Earthly sojourn, you will be blessed with inspired thoughts from your higher mind and the doors of manifestation will open up for you. You will be equipped with the power of discernment which means that you accept responsibility and know when to speak and when to be silent. The power of discernment will also mean that you will allow others to find their own truth in their own time. Remember that you are only responsible for your spiritual growth and well-being, aim to live the example that you wish to be. You will have the power of balance which means moderation in all things, and also means enjoying all the beauty of creation while radiating this beauty forth to all things. In this way the balance you attain will radiate harmony and peace. The power of transcendence means that through incorporating all the other areas of spiritual power, and radiating it forth that you will release and transcend your old limiting, controlling belief structures claiming all the gifts that are your divine birthright.

Through these areas of spiritual power, you begin to live and experience empowerment fearlessly embarking in unchartered territory, knowing you have the ability to succeed in whatever endeavor you choose to pursue, it also means mastering your ego and bringing your desires into harmony with your highest good and the highest good of all. When this occurs, you experience the power of transformation, which leads to peace, happiness, and beauty in all you seek within the realm of unity-consciousness.

We have discussed much this day dear One. Do you now understand the rationale for returning to the Earth for another sojourn?"

"Yes, it is a lot to take in, but I think after all that has been said here, that I have enough rationale to return to the Earth, with all the promises and all the trials and tribulations we discussed," the one formerly known as Michelle replied.

"We have outlined the things that are the most out of balance for you and thus the things that have caused you the most pain from your prior life. We think it best that you use these imbalances to create the life lessons, experiences, and situations that you bring into your next lifetime. If you agree, then your circle of angels, and guides will aid you in preparing for your next descent into the third dimension. We will provide you with the blessings you need before incarnating that will aid you in remembering that you are there for a purpose, a mission, for your highest good and the highest good of others and that we are with you every step of the way as you remember and begin to take your journey in returning Home. What do you think?" asks a guide.

"I think I am ready. Let's do this!" the one formerly known as Michelle replied excitedly and enthusiastically. "Here is to freedom!"

www.ingramcontent.com/pod-product-compliance
Lightning Source LLC
Chambersburg PA
CBHW031322040426
42443CB00005B/188